How To Make A Movie

A Few Secrets

By

Sumner Jules Glimcher

Note To Reader

This book was originally published electronically as an EBOOK. Originally the intent was to have the book self-contained with excerpts from my documentaries embedded as part of the book to be read on an EREADER. The same stills and links to the excerpts are in this print version.

For readers who may be interested in acquiring a digital download or a DVD of an entire film, please visit www.amazon.com and search for "Sumner Jules Glimcher." Or visit www.westminsterproductions.com or email the author at sumner.glimcher@nyu.edu

How To Make A Movie
A Few Secrets

Prologue

Today, where simple video recording devices enable anyone to record images and sound easily and inexpensively, virtually anyone can create a film. This book is the primer that will raise the level of those films to professional status.

I have produced *and* directed some three dozen films in my lifetime ranging from nine minutes to one hour in length.   I have also taught filmmaking at Harvard, my alma mater, at Columbia University for a decade, and most recently at NYU. At New York University, I was the Director of the "*Department of Film, Video and Broadcasting*" at its School of Continuing Education where I was largely responsible for creating the finest film program on the East Coast. Many friends have asked me how to make a professional quality film. This book is intended to respond to that request.   It will teach you the craft of filmmaking; the art is up to you.

Every film is unique. Each film I have made presented a new challenge. I intend to walk you through some twenty of the films I have made.   A different film will illustrate each chapter. In each situation, I shall tell you exactly how and why I made that particular film. Then, if your tablet/e-reader supports it, you may be able to see an excerpt of that particular film. If you prefer reading a soft cover paperback without the film excerpts, you will be able to order a physical book online from any one of the name online book-sellers. In some situations, you may be able to download an entire film from one of the name online movie-sellers onto your computer or tablet.   By analyzing what was involved in making each of these films, you should learn by example how each situation was resolved.

Chapter Index

Planting & Transplanting Pruning Practices at The Brooklyn Botanic Garden

Early in my career I was asked to make a film on pruning by the Brooklyn Botanic Garden. This film was intended to be a "how to" piece to inform gardeners how to professionally prune trees, shrubs and plants. This film pleased its sponsors to the extent that I was then immediately asked to make another film on "Planting." To my utter amazement, both films won awards!

Never having had held a pair of pruning shears in my hand, I wondered where to begin. And here is where I should mention one of the most significant aspects of making documentaries.

Whenever making a new film, the filmmaker is learning something new. And as an individual who loves to learn, this aspect of my career enabled profound personal growth as I was forced to master the subject matter each time I accepted a new commission. Today I am a fairly accomplished gardener.

In many cases one makes a documentary film by plunging into the subject, i.e. filming what is going on and then creating the film in the cutting room. In these two situations, however, both pieces were to be very carefully scripted and then filmed, shot by shot. The illustrative material had to show just what the script would say. Thus, not having the slightest ideas how to prune anything, I went to the expert at hand; the chief gardener at the Garden. I turned on my tape recorder and asked her to take me, step by step, through the entire pruning process. If I didn't understand every bit of the process, I asked her to amplify that aspect until I had a clear explanation of how and why the process worked. I then sat down at my typewriter and rewrote my notes into a rough script, keeping in mind what shots would be required. After completing the script I made a shot list.

On a brilliantly sunny day after I had completed the rough script, I brought my cameraman to the Garden to begin photography. I had both the script and shot list with me. The Garden scheduled an expert gardener who had vast experience in planting and pruning. He was patient and accommodating in repeating the process so that we were able to record each step from several angles. Later in the editing room the different angles would enable us to cut from shot to shot to best show what he was doing.

I'd like to concentrate on one sequence i.e. how to plant a rose bush.

The gardener had arrived with a wheelbarrow, a shovel, a rose bush with bare roots, a pair of pruning shears and a bag of mulch. He began by digging a hole slightly larger than the bare roots of the rose bush. As he dug, he mounded up the soil around the perimeter of the hole. After the hole became slightly larger than the roots, he snipped off the ends of the roots so as to get a fresh end. Then he put one or two shovelfuls of soil into a small pyramid in the center of the hole, and placed the roots on the pyramid. After the bush was firmly standing, he filled in most of the hole with soil leaving about two inches from the top of the soil to the surface of the hole. He then mounded up all the leftover soil around the hole, and with a nearby hose, slowly filled in the freshly planted rose bush with water. Using his shoes, he gently tamped down the soil and when the water had been completely absorbed by the soil, once again added a little more water. He then filled in the remaining space to the top of the hole with what he called mulch. As he proceeded, he told us exactly what he was doing and why. With my portable audio tape deck, I recorded every word. And during the entire process, I asked my cameraman to shoot each step, and in each case from several angles. This entire sequence took several hours, and as the light faded, we wrapped up our gear and headed to a lab where we left the exposed negative to be processed. The next day, we picked up the processed negative and a color 16mm work print that had been exposed and processed. The work print was a positive made from the negative. That was what we work with in editing the final film.

-TECHNICAL DIVERSION- YOU NEED NOT READ THE NEXT SECTION TO LEARN HOW TO MAKE A MOVIE-

In those pre-digital days, we shot 16mm film. Eastman Kodak, the largest producer of motion picture footage in the United States, which was based in Rochester, New York, was the main producer of what was known as "raw stock," i.e. a base of cellulose acetate coated with what was known as the "emulsion." The cellulose acetate, a flexible strip of plastic that came in varying widths, was the base on which the emulsion was coated. This was all done in a darkroom since the emulsion was light sensitive. The width of the film varied from the smallest (8 millimeters) to 16mm, the size most used in documentaries to 35mm, the size most used for feature films and then later to 70mm for theatrical wide screens.

Film was loaded into light tight rolls or magazines of varying length. Sixteen-millimeter film was most commonly supplied in one hundred foot cans and also in one thousand foot magazines. There were some 16mm cameras that were most commonly used. One of the best was the Arriflex camera made in Germany with the usual fine

craftsmanship associated with German manufacturing. It came in both 16mm and 35 mm for theatrical films.

The French also made a fine camera, the Éclair.

In America there was a popular camera called the Bolex. Kodak also made several 16mm cameras.

The first camera I ever owned, purchased when just before I traveled to Germany in take a job at Radio Free Europe in 1954, was a Bell & Howell "Filmo."
Prior to the modern small, portable efficient batteries, you wound these cameras up with a key. This tightened a spring which, when you turned the cameras on, allowed the film to move through the camera at exactly 16 or 24 frames per second. The B&H FILMO had three turrets to hold three different lenses: a normal 50mm; a 75mm telephoto; and a 25mm wide angle. The 50mm lens provided a "normal" perspective; the telephoto made distant objects look larger; and the wide-angle was used to bring a wide perspective to the image. That is if one wanted to film an entire room in one shot, by using the wide-angle lens one could capture a wide perspective in one shot.

One purchased what was called "raw stock" or unexposed film from the Kodak warehouse on 72nd Street and York Avenue, loaded it into a camera and shot the "footage" required. You then took the exposed raw stock to a Film Laboratory where the film was developed. The latent image on the emulsion after being passed through a liquid chemical "developer" became real and one would see frame after frame of actual picture. The film was then passed though a "fixer" which preserved the image, and then hung on strips to dry.

After drying, the negative was run through a printer where a "positive" was exposed, then the positive underwent the same chemical process and now you had a "work print." From the late 1800s up until the mid 1900s, all film was black and white until color became the norm. And until modern lightweight batteries were invented, all motion picture footage was passed through cameras that were wound up with a spring that ran the film at 24 frames per second.

After creating a "work print" a film editor would cut each shot apart, then glue them together in the right order to properly tell the story. He or she would splice together the different shots on what was known as a "splicer" with special film cement. The work print was the basic visual element that was used to make the final film.

Sound Recording began on primitive wax cylinders by inventors such as Thomas Alva Edison. A microphone would pick up variations in sound, which would be transmitted mechanically to a needle, which would pass over a revolving wax cylinder, and the tiny variations would be transmitted in the depth of the soft wax. When the soft wax would be pressed against a hard "positive," it would create a record. When the record was played back the reverse process allowed you to hear the sound coming from a speaker. Soon electronic progress would replace the previous mechanical and modern sound tracks emerged.

In the early days of filmmaking there was a basic piece of equipment on which most films were edited called the Moviola.

This was a heavy, large awkward piece of equipment that had a spindle where one put a reel holding the work print, which was threaded through a viewer, and then would go to a take-up reel, which reeled in the film after having been seen in the viewer.

Adjacent to the film feed and take up reels which fed the film through the viewer, were the sound equivalents. Here, instead of film, however was a reel of Mylar tape which had an iron oxide emulsion. When recording sound, a microphone fed electronic variations to a sound head, which imprinted tiny variations on the iron oxide particles in the emulsion. In playing back the tape, when it was passed over a sound reading head, these tiny variations went to an amplifier to increase its volume, and thence to a speaker, which then translated this minute variation into variations on a coil that transformed these variation to actual sound waves. When synced together, one had the image and sound that made the final film. In making a simple film one had the image and one sound track, perhaps with narration on it. As filmmaking became more sophisticated, additional sound tracks (music, sound effects, etc,) could be laid in to create a rich and more complex final film.

When I was working at Radio Free Europe in the mid-fifties, one of our engineers returned from Switzerland with amazing news. A Polish Sound Engineer named Stefan Kudelski, had invented the first modern lightweight portable tape recorder called the Nagra.

The flexibility of newer lightweight cameras and the Nagra created a revolution for modern documentary filmmakers. The final element that completed today's transformation to modern documentary filmmaking was "crystal sync" which kept a camera and tape recorder in exact synchronization.

In the editing room the work print was put onto a 16mm reel and attached to the feed spindle of the Moviola, threaded through the viewer, which magnified the image, and attached onto the take-up reel. The Moviola was set to run at 24 frames per second. In an editing room is where a film is finally created. Extended from the picture part of the Moviola is another matching set of spindles. These feed and take-up reels, passed a piece of Mylar tape over a sound head. The Mylar tape had a metallic coating of iron oxide which, having previously been passed over a sound head from which it received on the metallic coating, sound pulses which organized the metallic particles in the iron oxide into a specific organization. When this tape was passed over a sound reader, it recreated the exact sound (music, narration, sound effects) which had been recorded when the filmmaker recorded a narrator recording the final script.

One then added another sound head to the Moviola for the music. Since these two elements, picture and sound are kept exactly in sync by perforations; they correspond precisely so that the sound is in perfect sync with the image. We start the first shot of this sequence to its corresponding piece of narration. That continues until we have finished cutting the entire film.

-PLEASE RESUME HERE-

Now to continue with the non-technical aspects of making our film, we then added shots we had planned for opening titles and closing credits. I chose vast fields of spring daffodils, evoking "Dr. Zhivago." Meanwhile several other elements were proceeding. I had made up a list of opening titles and closing credits, which I had brought to a "Title House." Here a facility, using its vast array of varying fonts and type faces created the titles and credits and recorded them on film and gave us finished material.

Since I always use either original music or indigenous sound for my sound tracks, I had hired a colleague, Arnold Gamson, a talented composer/conductor to whom I had shown the "rough cut" as we were editing. As we watched the film going through a projector I told Arnold the kind of music I wanted for each sequence, the instrumentation, etc. For the rose planting sequence I decided that I wanted a live clarinet, and after the planting sequence, we segued to a stunning series of close-ups of perfectly blossoming roses which we shot some months later.

To me, music is one of the most vital elements of any film. In this case I hired Stanley Drucker, Chief Clarinetist of the New York Philharmonic and scheduled two hours in a recording studio. There I screened the finished rose planting sequence and as he watched, the clarinetist played the most thrilling arpeggio, which so matched the visual images that it is one of the most perfect matches in any of the films I have ever made. Please watch and listen as you play this coming sequence.

"Planting & Transplanting: Pruning at the Brooklyn Botanical Garden"

Produced & Directed by Sumner Jules Glimcher
http://youtu.be/RiIzlx8kWWw

For another example of how music can elevate a film, listen to Jay Ungar's music in Ken Burn's "Civil War" series.

A Look Back

For me, it is imperative to know, understand and appreciate how the making of documentary films began, grew, and became what it is today. Since much of its history makes a good story, you may enjoy knowing it as well.

Around the turn of the last century, circa the late 1800s and early 1900s, still photography, which had begun some hundred years earlier, evolved into motion pictures. This was due to a phenomenon called "persistence of vision." It was learned that if a series of still images, each moving slightly with a tiny continuous progressive change in each image, when seen rapidly, such as by flipping quickly through the pages of a book, appeared to actually "move." Names such as Edison in America, Lumiere and Pathe in France, and others combined to create a camera, which took still images at a rate of 16 or 24 frames per second, and when these still images were projected at the same rate, the still images appeared to move. A true story was that at the turn of the last century when a short black and white film was projected in a Paris Theater as an approaching train on the screen became lager and larger the entire audience screamed in terror and dashed from the theater!

These early movies were silent until the advent of "The Jazz Singer," starring Al Jolson in 1929, when sound was added. Story telling by film became one of the most popular means of mass entertainment and education ever conceived.

A key figure in the development of early film in America was a man named Robert Flaherty (1884-1951), who was frequently called the "father of the documentary." Flaherty was an iron explorer who worked in Hudson's Bay, Canada. As he prepared to make one of his exploratory trips north, his boss, Sir William Mackenzie, suggested that Flaherty take along a motion picture camera. Flaherty brought with him a 35mm hand-cranked camera, and he was so intrigued by the life of the native Inuit people that he began to neglect his real work and spent most of his time recording these natives. He returned to Toronto with 30,000 feet of 35 mm film.

A heavy drinker and smoker, while editing this footage he dropped a lit cigarette into his editing bin where the highly combustible nitrate footage quickly exploded. He lost all the film and was badly burned himself.

Determined to make a new and better film, in 1920, he returned north and with funds supplied by the French fur trading company, "Revillon Freres," and once again began to photograph the natives. He selected a typical family: Nanook the father, his wife and children and recorded them in their daily lives.

He also brought along complete developing, printing and projection equipment so that he could see his processed film as he worked. He could also show the Inuit the film as well. While living in a cabin next to the Revillon Freres warehouse, it is said that he had an affair with Nanook's wife and fathered a boy whom he never acknowledged.

He returned to Toronto a year later and released "Nanook of the North" in 1922. This silent film with sub-titles told the story of Nanook's life and became a worldwide sensation. Flaherty made three more films: "Moana," a coming of age film in Samoa in 1926; "Man of Aran" in 1934; and "Louisiana Story," his only sound film in 1948. The music for Louisiana Story was composed by Virgil Thompson, and is a perfect example of how an original score can enhance a stunning film. Flaherty's cameraman on the latter film was, a youth named Richard "Ricky" Leacock. Leacock later became another pioneer in documentaries when he partnered with D.A. Pennebaker. David and Albert Maysles also did pioneering work in producing "Gimme Shelter" "Salesman" and "Grey Gardens."

Although I never met Flaherty, a larger than life legend in his lifetime, in the early 1960's I met his widow, Frances. Frances had worked with her husband in all his latter three films and I became a Trustee of the Foundation she formed to perpetuate his work. In 1967 and 1968 I was the Seminar Director for two annual Flaherty Seminars and I met and worked with many other seminal figures in documentaries. I knew and worked with Pennebaker, Leacock, pioneers in what became known as 'direct cinema.' Al Maysles, whom the NEW YORK TIMES calls "the greatest documentary filmmaker alive," remains one of my closest colleagues.

Hiroshima-Nagasaki, August 1944

During my lifetime I have produced a few significant films. In some situations I have also been involved in some dramatic occasions. The story about making the film above was simply amazing!

One day in 1970, while I was the Manager of the Center For Mass Communication at Columbia University, I received a letter from a Professor of Law at Tokyo University. The letter said that nine Japanese newsreel cameramen had arrived at Hiroshima the day after the atomic bomb had exploded over that city, did the same at Nagasaki, and remained to continue to record, on 35mm black and white film, the devastation in the two cities, and the sufferings if the people who were present. As most of the world now knows, after the initial bombing which killed hundreds of thousands of people instantly, some time afterwards, people who had been exposed to the explosions some miles way and not been killed, began to develop something called "radiation sickness." These Japanese cameramen recorded it all.

After the Japanese surrender, when General MacArthur occupied the Islands of Japan and saw this footage he felt that it was so horrifying that it should be withheld from the public and marked it "Top Secret." So it remained until I received this letter.

My journalistic instincts caused me to believe that honest exposure, rather than hiding unpleasant facts should dictate policy, so I decided to follow up. I wrote the US Government asking about this footage. They responded and said that no such footage existed and stonewalled all my efforts to admit its existence. I persisted for months and not until I asked for the intercession of our two New York senators, was I finally told that the footage did, indeed, exist, and if I came to Washington I could screen it. I set a date, took AMTRAK to DC, where at the National Archives I sat through four hours of some of the most terrifying film footage I had ever seen. Because of the publicity I had generated the footage was declassified and I was able to order a duplicate negative and work print. A few weeks later this arrived at my CMC office. I had decided to make a documentary out of this most unique footage.

I appointed my colleague, Erik Barnouw, the Editor of CMC as my Producer, and Paul Ronder, one of our more talented film students as Editor. I also appointed Geoff Bartz, another young student (now the top Editor at HBO) as Assistant Editor and we all went to work. We ended up some months later with a 16-minute documentary unlike any film ever seen. Paul wrote and read a simple, underplayed narration. A female Japanese student also spoke a dramatic sequence. Instead of music another student played a high pitched single note that, as the film progressed, kept getting higher in pitch.

I had an enormous argument with Erik, which caused me to make one of the biggest mistakes in my career. When Paul did the final sound mix, the sound track was badly distorted and I, as Executive Producer, suggested that we remix the program. Erik, in a rush to see it released, vetoed my suggestion. Since he was fifteen years my senior and a person I had great respect for, regretfully I acceded to his request, but since I did not want my name associated with anything less than the best, in a fit of pique, took my title as Executive Director off the final credits. So when the film became known as a worldwide sensation, Erik ended up getting all the credit! Later on when CMC was dissolved MOMA took over its distribution and fixed the sound track. It now resides in the National Archive without my name as Executive Producer. And if it had not been for me, the film would never have been made. Sic Gloria Transit Mundi!

One example of the significance of this work was an editorial written by the Boston Globe. "This documentary is probably the most important documentary made in this century."

Here is the opening of the film from my own private copy where I restored my title as the Executive Producer.

"Hiroshima-Nagasaki: August, 1944"
Executive Producer Sumner Jules Glimcher
http://youtu.be/CUAmDQFXa4M

North From Mexico

This film, made around the same time as "Hiroshima," could not have been more different, and making it totally changed my life. It all began at a cocktail party one weekend in Westport, Connecticut where I was then living. I met a fellow named Harold Mason, and as one does at a party, he asked me what I did and I asked him the same. It turned out that Harold was the President and CEO of a paperback reprint publishing company named Greenwood Press. When I told him I worked at the Center for Mass Communication at Columbia University where I made educational films, his eyes lit up.

He told me that Greenwood had recently reprinted a paperback titled "North From Mexico" written by Carey McWilliams and that the book described how the

Conquistadores, Francisco Vasquez Coronado, with a party made up of Spaniards, Native-American Indians and Mexicans traveled 'North from Mexico' in an attempt to find the legendary seven cities of gold. Coronado who was then in Mexico, mounted his expedition north in 1540.

McWilliams, then the editor of "The Nation," had grown up in the American Southwest and had always been fascinated by how our west had been settled. Harold told me that at that time, when African-Americans had begun to explore their own history, "Chicanos" the descendants of the early explorers of our American west. had also begun to make their history better known to "Anglo" Americas. This book did a splendid job in portraying that segment of our history.

Harold said that the book was popular in schools, particularly in the southwest where most Chicanos lived. He wondered if a film, based on the book, might stimulate book sales? And then he asked if I might be able to produce a film? I asked him to get me a copy to read which he did, and it became instantly obvious that such a film, all to be shot in one of the most colorful and glorious parts of our southwest, would be a delightful assignment. So Greenwood Press commissioned the work and one of the most interesting projects in my career commenced.

Once the contract was signed, I visited McWilliams in the editorial office of "The Nation." He was delighted to learn of my assignment and gave me the names and telephone numbers of many of his friends and colleagues who lived in New Mexico and Arizona, the two states in which most of the photography would be done.

At that time, prior to writing the scripts for the films I was making myself, I still used other writers for the films I would be making. Thus I asked one of my fellow teachers at Columbia, Harold Flender, to write the film, and he accepted. Harold was a talented scriptwriter with a wild sense of humor and this would be the first of two films that we made together. Summer was approaching which made our teaching load at Columbia less demanding, so we scheduled a two-week scouting trip, which would begin in El Paso, New Mexico and end in Santa Fe. I booked our flights; reserved a rental car and began to call the several numbers McWilliams had given me. Our itinerary called for us to meet our first contact at the University of Texas in El Paso, then drive north, following the Rio Grande, as Coronado had done, stopping at various significant sites along the way. Two weeks driving north in New Mexico with one of the most interesting travel companions I ever knew was a fabulous way to start this new adventure.

One of the first names we had been given by McWilliams was that of Professor Philip Ortego at UTEXAS who taught Chicano History, and he became not only one of our most important sources, but ultimately the narrator of the film. Philip was, as McWilliams had already been, a vast source of new information. We spent hours with him taking copious notes. The following morning we headed north to our next destination, White Sands, New Mexico, a brilliantly shimmering stretch of desert, which was also one of the sites for US Government research on rockets. Route 25, which criss-crossed the river (the "Rio Bravo del Norde," as the natives called it), in those days was virtually our own private highway. Soon we approached a handsome villa, built of native adobe bricks where we were given a royal welcome by the Western artist and sculptor, Peter Hurd and his charming wife, Henriette, the daughter of the famed Pennsylvania artist, NC Wyeth. Peter and Henriette were not only generous hosts (we stayed overnight with them) but later we would interview them for the film and shoot many sequences in and around their authentic Spanish Hacienda. Our road trip ended in Santa Fe which became our home base as we ventured to nearby landmarks.

Santa Fe in 1970 was a simple and gracious town much removed from the crowded, tourist-ridden Santa Fe of today. Aside from its many original homes all built in hacienda style out of adobe bricks, there were many locations nearby which Harold I marked for later photography. There were unique locations, each within a short drive that we would return to film. To the west was Bandelier National Monument, a series of tall cliffs made out of stone so porous that the Native Americans had, for generations, enlarged these small caves into livable homes. At the bottom of the cliffs were kivas whose stone remains are now visited by the descendants of the earlier natives. To the north was an authentic Native-American village called Taos. When we were there this tiny adobe village was alive with Native-Americans; but now a 'quaint' tourist attraction where one must pay an entrance fee to take pictures!

To the East was an early Christian church built by the Coronado expedition, known as the "Pecos National Monument." As Harold wrote in his script, "the Conquistadores came not only with pick and shovel, but also with cross and crucifix to convert the natives. Who is to say which were the more "civilized?"

Simply driving around one day a few miles from town we came upon another small town, Espanola, which had a magnificent church, which we knew we would film. Months later, when I returned with my shooting crew, we saw a caravan of Hollywood trucks, a film crew and of all people, Paul Newman! Paul was shooting a western. He had a crew of fifty-five, five of whom were simply the wranglers to handle the herd of Black Angus.

That night Harold and I went to the best steak house in town. In the booth next to us were half a dozen of Newman's crew chatting and laughing about the day's events. Newman came by, chatted with the crew for a while, and then entered a private dining room at the rear. Harold suggested I ask Newman to narrate our film, and never one to ignore a challenge, I decided to try. I entered the back room where a glowering heavy-set guy in a black mustache told me I was interrupting a private dinner. "I know," I said, "but I wanted a word with my neighbor, Paul." Paul and Joanna had recently moved into a large old barn in Westport. I walked directly to Paul, introduced myself, told him I was making a documentary on the settlement of the old west and asked him if would consider doing the narration? Certainly, he said, drop me a line when you are ready. Alas, three months later when we were ready to record the narration and I wrote him he sent back a short note:

"Dear Sumner,

I'm leaving tomorrow to edit my own film in LA and will not be back for the next two months.

So sorry,

Paul"

Next came another hair-raising adventure! Harold and I had been told of an ancient gold mine and Harold's script called for an old wooden mine shaft that the Chicanos might have used a century ago when the Chicanos worked the mines. We drove south to a tiny village called Cerillos ("Little Hills."). There we went to an address we had been given to obtain directions to this mine. Soon we were bumping along a rutted dirt road far off the main paved roads twisting and turning until we approached a very large sign which read," **NO TRESPASSING! PRIVATE LAND!**" Harold and I looked at each other; I shrugged my shoulders and stepped on the gas. Shortly we came to an extraordinary scene. There, right in front of us, stood a real working mine with a wooden mine shaft, exactly what we were seeking! There was a chimney belching smoke and several cars parked in front of the mineshaft. I pulled up next to the cars and saw, off on a hill to my left, a small cabin. As Harold and I each opened our doors and exited the car Harold said to me, softly, " Don't make any sudden moves. There is a guy with a rifle pointed directly at us looking out one of the windows."

I figured that boldness was probably a better approach than turning tail. I slowly and deliberately began to climb the hill, Harold walking beside me. The rifle never wavered. As we got about a hundred yards from the cabin, a loud voice yelled, "Stop right where you are! Who are you? What do you want?"

There have been times when I paid little attention to a comment, but this was not one of them. Both Harold and I stopped in our tracks. I responded by telling the inhabitants of the cabin that Harold and I were University Professors from Columbia, that we were unarmed and could we please enter and talk with them?

There was some talk inside, the rifle was lowered and we were told to proceed. There were four guys in the cabin; three roughly dressed as miners and the fellow in charge, a city dressed fellow in a suit and tie. The guy in charge introduced himself as Jack, and asked us what we wanted? Harold and I showed him our Columbia University IDs, which he scrutinized carefully. I told him about our film project and that we needed to film an ancient wooden mineshaft, similar to those used by Chicanos a couple of hundred years ago.

Jack laughed and said that if there was anything they did not need it was any kind of publicity. They had found an old mine which was still spewing forth gold. There was no way in the world would they allow us to take pictures!

Here I was in a quandary; the perfect object to shoot to illustrate the script, and they, with good reason, had no reason to allow us to do so! I explained that we would shoot the mine shaft in close-up so that anyone seeing the film could have no idea of were it was. Jack did not seem convinced, but much to my surprise, the foreman of the miners, a friendly guy named Tony, came to our support. If we did as we said, he agreed, no one would ever know the location. And if we gave our word never to disclose where we had been, what harm would it do? His support did the trick, and Jack agreed to allow us to return at a later date to shoot. When we returned a few months later, not only did we get excellent footage of the mine shaft, but Tony took us underground and showed us with his pick, how he chopped a chunk of ore, with its glittering specks of gold, right out of the walls. The mining sequence was terrific.

But how did this film change my life? Are you ready for an amazing story? When we completed "North From Mexico," its release and subsequent publicity did exactly what Mason had wanted. Sales of both the film and the book soared. Mason was thrilled. One day he asked me to lunch.

In addition to his day job as CEO of Greenwood Press; Harold's hobby was collecting antiquarian books. He told me that he had recently made some money by selling a library of antiquarian books and was seeking a tax shelter. Harold was far more knowledgeable in financial matters than I. He had by then, also become fascinated by filmmaking and asked if I might be interested in quitting my job at Columbia, which would mean no more commuting, and starting a film making company in Westport, if it were properly financed? If so, how much money would I need?

Since my salary at Columbia was based upon how much income I produced, and I was successful in that, I was then, in 1970 earning about $25,000 per year. Much more than the usual academic salary. So I told Harold that I would need two year's salary; $50,000, plus another $50,000 to produce a beginning library of educational material to sell. Or a total of $100,000. To my utter astonishment, Harold took out a checkbook and wrote out a check to me for $100,000! You could have knocked me over with a feather! One hundred thousand dollars in 1970 was perhaps the equivalent of half a million dollars today. That is how making "North From Mexico," changed my life. I gave Columbia two weeks notice, found an office in Westport on which I signed a lease, purchased some furniture and equipment, and began the next chapter of my life.

However to get back to the real reason I am writing about "North From Mexico" in talking about "How to make a Movie," I want you to see the power of the "Montage." In order to put you quickly in the proper frame of mind the opening montage in this film consists of a series of "Chicano faces" put to the right music. I recorded the faces in Cuidad Juarez in Mexico and the music of a Mariachi band much later in Santa Fe.

Please look and listen.

"North From Mexico"
Produced & Directed by Sumner Jules Glimcher
http://youtu.be/K8GxhHC_rXE

A Problem of Power

There were several interesting aspects in making this film, and much to learn. It was sponsored by the National Council of Churches. It was a year before I would be leaving Columbia, while I was still then the Manager of the Center for Mass Communication at Columbia University Press. The Council, each year, would choose an important topic for churches all around America to focus on for the following year. "Poverty in Latin America" would be the topic for the upcoming year and Bill Fore, the Manager of the Council, suggested that they finance a film that could be used to kick off discussions at different churches. He asked me to come to a meeting to talk about how CMC might help. Since our mandate was to produce and distribute educational films, mostly for nonprofits, CMC appeared to be an appropriate production unit to help the Council.

When Bill and I met, there were three other people in the room; a fellow named Herb Lowe, another named Bill Wipfler and a woman named Laura Hogan. Bill began by saying that while they had a reasonable budget for a forty-five minute film shot on location, there would be some limitations. First and foremost was that that we would be limited to just one country, although that country must be representative of all of South America. After some discussion they told me that they felt that Colombia represented most of Latin America in that it was neither the largest nor the smallest, neither the richest nor the poorest, and in many ways clearly a nation that might be seen as being sort of in the middle.

My reputation as a producer director had convinced Fore that I could make the film he wanted. Wipfler was one of the Council's most expert advisors on Latin America, was fluent in Spanish and had many personal contacts in Colombia. He was selected by the Council to be the focus of the film in that he would do all the interviewing in both languages. Hogan, while not expert in any of these aspects, was nevertheless to be the Council's representative and would go on location with us. Herb Lowe was to be the Executive Producer and was to be my main contact with the Council.

I needed to find a bi-lingual cinematographer and went to my friends at the United Nations. Not surprisingly they introduced me to a young man named Gustavo Nieto-Roa. Not only was Gustavo fluent in Spanish as well as English, but also as a native of Bogota, he would be perfect for the job. I asked Warren Johnson, my long-time cinematographer for earlier projects, if we would serve as sound recordist, and also operate the second camera. And so Nieto-Roa with his Éclair, and Johnson with his ARRI and Nagra, comprised my tech crew. Laura would come along as the representative of the Council. I planned a four-week trip for the five of us, booked flights and hotel accommodations in Bogota and we set off for what turned out to be a fascinating assignment.

Our first challenge arose at the airport when we deplaned in Bogota. As I recall we had some twelve or thirteen pieces of luggage. In addition to a personal bag for each, we carried one Éclair sound camera, one ARRIFLEX, one Nagra tape recorder, one large box of one hundred 100 foot rolls of Kodak negative film, one Lowel light kit, one box of ¼" tapes, another container full of filters, spare lenses, gaffer tape, extension cords and other paraphernalia. Not what customs deemed the usual luggage for a group of tourists? Why were we carrying all this filmmaking equipment? Were we planning to sell it in Colombia?

I had earlier determined that we would plan and carry out our project under the radar. Since we anticipated that our resulting film would most likely be critical of the regime, our plan was to appear to be a "film class" (I had my Columbia University ID). We were planning to make a film to promote tourism in Colombia. And so the five of us sat in the customs office while a group of airport officials sat in a room and discussed the situation. We had to appear carefree, but inside I knew that the success or failure of our mission might just reside with these customs officials discussing our mission.

About half an hour later the chief came outside and waved us through!

At first, we began by checking our equipment while Wipfler was on the 'phone setting up appointments. He connected with an American missionary whom we were able to interview on the second day. We sprang into action as Jim, the American Protestant Missionary, who had lived and worked in Bogota for more than two decades, told us about the complex relationships between America and the Colombians. This interview, one of the few in English, later opened the film and set the stage for what was later revealed. Jim told us that the most innovative changes of the present were being made by a group of rebel Roman Catholic Priests.

As a result of the excellence of Wipfler's contacts, by the third day we were booked day and night with interviews. Our second meeting was with Father Rene Garcia, who we were then introduced to as a friend of Jim's. Garcia became the 'voice' of the film and the most significant symbol of the "Problem of Power."

We learned that there were four pillars of power in the community: the government, the church, the rich, and the military. They made up about 3% of the nation, and ruled the land. The middle class, that is the people who did the work of the nation, lived in the cities and made up 12% of the population, the remaining 85%, that is to say the masses, were the poor most of who lived on the land and tilled the ground.

Garcia took us to the barrios, those horrible places in the cities, where the desperate poor squatted on hills so that raw sewage (they had no toilets) could flow downhill. We interviewed rich landowners, rich politicians, a wonderful guy with a sense of responsibility who ran public TV and a ghastly woman who ran a for-profit commercial TV. Most affecting were the poor people who tried to earn a living by working the worn out land. Our challenge was how to present the Spanish of most of those we interviewed into the English we needed for our American audiences.

After our return, in the editing room, I decided to keep the voices of all our interviewees since their passion was so important. Thus at the start of each interview I kept the original sound in Spanish for several seconds so as to establish the emotional validity of the speaker. After a full sentence or two I then dropped the volume and completed the interview in English while still keeping the original Spanish in the back ground. To do that I went once again to the UN and auditioned dozens of speakers to try find voices that would appear to be the natural voices of the interviewees we saw on screen. I thought that this would be preferable to sub-titles and leave you to decide if I made the right decision. To demonstrate, here are several sequences.

Here is Senor Salzmann, one of my heroes!

"A Problem Of Power"
Produced & Directed by Sumner Jules Glimcher
http://youtu.be/ldmZa_TqNH8

One of the most interesting conversations we had was when we decided to climb up a mountain to interview a family who had a tiny plot of land at the top of a mountain. On a footpath at the bottom of the mountain we came across a family which was so articulate that we decided to have them in the film. Bill asked the grandfather about money that they were supposed to receive from the United States.

His answer astounded us!!!!

"A Problem Of Power"
Produced & Directed by Sumner Jules Glimcher
http://youtu.be/SKFruXfNp_w

I believe that by keeping all the original Spanish in the background, each interview maintains all the passion of the speaker, thus maintaining the integrity if the film that would have been lost if we used sub-titles. It is one of my favorite films. What do you think?

Alberto Giacometti

I'm a bit embarrassed to tell you that as much as I love art, I only made two films featuring art and artists. However the Giacometti film was such a pure delight, that it makes up for the lack of quantity. Like many of my other works, it also came about as a pure accident. In this chapter I am going to discuss more about narration.

I had just come from a meeting with Willard van Dyke, then the director of Film at MOMA (Museum of Modern Art). As one of his curators walked me to the door, she asked if I had seen their Giacometti exhibit. I had not. It was such an extensive retrospective, she told me, that it should be documented with a film. She asked if, perhaps, CMC might want to make such a film? She knew that we had few funds at CMC and that MOMA also had no production money. But, she said, if it might help, she could arrange for the Museum to stay open and lit for one or two nights without cost to CMC if we might be able to document the exhibit.

Although I had never understood his tall, gaunt figures, I had always loved them so at the next meeting of the CMC Faculty Advisory Committee I brought up the idea of our self-funding such a project. Using our own film equipment and hiring a couple of students, I determined that we could make such a film for a modest sum.

At that time I had known a number of talented Columbia faculty and had asked half a dozen of them to serve as Faculty Advisors to help guide CMC through its existence. We met monthly and their combined knowledge and judgment were invaluable to CMC's success. To my surprise and delight, my committee staffed by such brilliant intellectuals as Harry Shapiro (Anthropologist), Telford Taylor (Lawyer and former Nuremburg Prosecutor), Maurie Rosenberg (Constitutional Lawyer), and Henry Graff (Presidential Historian) apparently all lovers of Giacometti's work enthusiastically endorsed the idea! One week later I took one of our more talented students, Stuart Chasmar, and an old silent ARRIFLEX camera and several rolls of film to the museum where we went from room to room shooting shots of all his work. His earliest work consisted of drawings, and then paintings and only late in his career did his elongated statues bring him fame. We spent two nights and captured all his work on film.

I had a treasure trove of images and needed a narration to tie the images together. What to do? In doing research on him I found that he had written several short pages on his work. They were, of course, in French since although born in Switzerland near the northern Italian border; he spent almost his entire working life in Paris. His wife, Annette and his brother Diego, were his chief models. I collected all of his writing I could find, had it all translated into English and then on one sunny weekend, took it all to the beach where I studied what he had written. When I put it into chronological order, it was as if the sun had come out!

As I read it chronologically, it appeared that the evolution of his artistic development shone through. How his primitive drawings led to paintings, which led to sculpture. His first tiny figures then emerged into huge slender, emaciated statues. I couldn't wait to get to the typewriter to reassemble his disjointed scribbling into a clear road map. Before the weekend was over, I had a real script! Now to the editing room. Stuart began to cut shots and spliced them to fit my script. In one day we had edited the images to fit the words! The finished piece ran just sixteen minutes.

The next day I brought my composer/conductor friend, Arnold Gamson, to watch the rough cut with me. I suggested the orchestration and the style of music I thought complementary to the work. A week later he had written a score for harp and harpsichord. We booked a recording studio, and two musicians, and we recorded the music he had written to a playback of the film. The final piece, with incredible images, fascinating sound and a narration that clearly spoke to his artistic development, made a work for which I have always been exceedingly proud. Evidently others appreciated it as well as the Edinburgh Film Festival thought so highly of it that they insisted that we blow the 16mm film up to 35mm where it was featured in one of the most exclusive Film Festivals of the world. The highest praise came when several viewers told me that after seeing the film, they understood his work.

Here is the film in its entirety.

"Alberto Giacometti"
Produced by Sumner Jules Glimcher
http://youtu.be/aqQyK3pI8lU

Golden Heritage, Golden Harvest

In this chapter we are going to talk about how aerial photography can enrich a film. Almost all films are shot from a single perspective and when projected, appear flat. Three D has been tried in different guises, usually to be seen with special glasses.

A far more effective result may be obtained by using aerial photography. Scenes shot from an airplane give real depth and perspective to any sequence. In my film, "North From Mexico," which I described earlier, I rented a high winged monoplane from the Santa Fe Airport for a morning and we flew over hundreds of miles recording the land, rivers, mountains and forests just a few hundred feet off the ground. Kivas, Bandelier National Monument and the 'Rio Bravo del Norde's' glistening waves all took on a magical aspect when cutting from the ground to aerial photography.

In my experience, propeller planes or small jets are superior to helicopters because of they vibrate less. And while an airplane rental adds to a budget, one saves much in terms of huge distances covered by air. In just the few hours we flew that day we went over much of New Mexico, shot the headwaters of rivers in other states to the north, and dipped down to scan an enormous open pit copper mine in over southern Arizona. Any aerial shot becomes a fantastic wide-angle lens!

While shooting "North From Mexico" however, there was a serious downside. Warren Johnson, my very talented cinematographer, became violently airsick. Since the pilot was otherwise occupied who was left to point the camera down?

The film I am choosing to show the benefits of aerial photography was a film I was hired to produce for the Government of Taiwan. It was titled, "Golden Heritage, Golden Harvest." And the story that led up to its production is worth telling.

As you read in the Chapter on North From Mexico, Harold and I had adjacent desks in our Westport office and the phone rang. I picked it up and Harold heard just my part of the conversation wherein I stated that I was sorry that I could not meet the caller since I would be going out to town. When I cradled the phone he said he did not know that I was going out of town. I told him that I was not going away, but did not want to meet the guy who had called. He asked me why and

I told him that the caller, a man who introduced himself as Gene Loh, represented the Republic of China and he wanted to talk with me about producing a film on Taiwan.

Harold looked puzzled since it appeared that our newly formed company was turning away business, so I continued. I told Harold that I detested Chiang Kai-shek, and would certainly not want to make a propaganda film for him about Taiwan.

To place this in political perspective, this was soon after Nixon and Kissinger had signed the Shanghai Communiqué. It was apparent that Taiwan would soon lose the "China Seat' at the UN and obviously Lohs' need for a film to keep the goodwill of the US was clearly apparent.

Harold stood up, out his hands on his hips, looked at me as if I was an idiot child and said:

"Sumner. Did I just give you one hundred thousand dollars to start this new company?"

"Yes."

"And are we assuming that this guy wants to pay us to make a film?"

"Yes."

"And can we use the money?"

"Certainly."

"Will you please do me a favor? Can you meet with him and see if

perhaps we can make his film without destroying your political imperatives? What can you lose by a meeting?"

Sheepishly I agreed. I called Loh back, told him that I had rearranged my schedule, and we made a lunch date for the following day. We met at a Chinese restaurant, Loh ordered by writing our choices in Chinese on a notepad, sat back and said:

"I've done some research and I know a little about you. I think you are one of those Harvard intellectuals who think more of the communists on the mainland than Chiang Kai-shek."

I sat quietly, astonished by his words..

"What you probably do not know is that when Chiang settled in Taiwan, he bought all the land and leased it to the peasants cheaply so that they could own their own land. He has changed his political philosophy completely.

"We need a documentary describing how the new Taiwan works. You will be free to travel and shoot whatever you want, provided, how ever, that you do not get involved in politics. Your film will not be censored. And we will pay you handsomely!"

I was flabbergasted. This was an offer I could not refuse. I told him that I would need to talk with my partner, agree on a budget and we agreed to meet a few days later to sign a contract. When I returned and told Harold the results he was delighted. And I certainly learned a lesson.

Since Taiwan badly wanted to have this film made, I decided to push the envelope. I had known that when Chiang left the mainland, he had taken every piece of art that was not nailed down. Essentially that meant everything but the architecture. He established "The National Palace Museum" in Taipei, the capital. I had always loved what I knew of Chinese art. I suggested to Harold that we ask Loh if they would allow us to make a film on that Museum. And also that they pay for it. Harold agreed; provided that this request would not endanger the first film they wanted. I called Gene and suggested that we sign a two-film agreement. He said he would cable Taipei with my request and let me know. Two days later we had a contract to make both films. I was ecstatic!

I brought with me a two-person crew. Warren Johnson, my sometimes-airsick cinematographer; and my wife Joan. I had for many years suggested that my wife begin to write narration. Prior to the times when I began to write narration myself I had usually hired writers, but now that our children were grown. I thought that instead of paying an outsider to write my films, if my wife wrote them we could keep the writer's fee within the family.

We landed at the Taipei Airport and transferred to the Grand Hotel; a glorious series of Chinese pavilions designed by Madame Chiang. While mentioning Madame Chiang, please allow me a short digression. I must recommend an astonishing book titled "The Soong Dynasty," written by Sterling Seagraves. I was so impressed by Seagrave's book that I began a long correspondence with him. As a result of writing this amazing history and threats on his life, he was hidden in Southern France, so we never met, but this is a book that any literate person must read. Here is a short summary.

Charlie Soong, the pater familius and founder of "The Soong Dynasty" was born in Hainan in 1863. Befriended by American missionaries, he was graduated from Vanderbilt University and started life as a missionary himself, but soon became a wealthy businessman. He met and became friendly with Sun Yat-sen and was deeply involved in the 1911 revolution in China. He and his wife had three daughters; Ai-ling, Ching-ling and Mei-ling, and two sons: TL and TA. All three girls attended Wesleyan College. Charlie died in 1918, aged 55.

What made the Soong family one of the powerhouses of the world were their marriages. Ai-ling married HH Kung, one of the wealthiest men in China. Ching-ling married Sun Yat-sen. And Meil-ing married Chiang Kai-shek! The power of these three women is certainly a startling case of truth being stranger than fiction. You must read this book.

Back to GHGH. If you ever saw the film: "Eat, Drink, Man, Woman" directed by Ang Lee, a native of Taiwan, (as well as alumnus from NYU Film School), it was shot at the Grand Hotel kitchen. Its Dining Room is where I first tasted genuine Chinese cuisine. I was told that when Chiang was forced off the mainland and ended up in Taiwan he brought with him the richest of the rich from the mainland and, of course they all brought their chefs! For the rest of our stay in Taiwan, the Grand dining room was my where I enjoyed the finest Chinese cuisine I ever eaten. I feature their dining room in two of my films.

"Golden Heritage, Golden Harvest"
Produced & Directed by Sumner Jules Glimcher
http://youtu.be/MBM_dIRwKyQ

The sequence in this film shot from the air was another adventure in itself. The government had bent over backward during our month long stay and towards the end I decided that several aerial shots could greatly enhance the photography. Since this was an island surrounded by seas, fishing, shipping and other maritime activities were central to our film, and to the lives of the island inhabitants.

Since our arrival, we had been assigned a government guide-interpreter who made our lives pleasant and efficient. I asked him if he could arrange a government helicopter for a full day and lo, the next day we were asked when? I selected a day and on that day, Warren and I, along with our guide-interpreter, departed for the airport, leaving Joan in the hotel to work on the script.

We climbed aboard a US Bell 'copter that seated five: pilot and co-pilot in front, and interpreter, Warren and me in the back. We flew over several ports and saw ships being built, fishermen on the shores and in boats, and flew to the southernmost tip of the island where in Kaoshung we flew over shipyards where decommissioned ships were being broken apart for their steel.

Hours later on our way home we approached the Karaoke Gorge where a mountain pass allowed passage from one side of the island to the other. It occurred to me that flying over this pass might provide some interesting footage so I asked our interpreter to ask the pilot to do so. Ever obliging we turned to starboard and began to climb as the mountains became higher. As we rose, it became evident that the thinner air was causing some stress to our aircraft as we climbed higher and higher. Now clouds had moved in and as we approached the summit, the pilot and copilot began to jabber excitedly as they pointed to the instrument panel. Our guide, whose face had turned a ghastly white, told us that we were running low on gas! Warren threw up and handed me the camera. I had never thought that I might die crashing on a mountaintop while on location in Taiwan, but there it was!

In the next moment, a miracle occurred: the clouds broke completely, we were flying over the ocean and the sky was clear blue as far as we could see. We had overshot the island, the pilot pulled a quick 180 and in minutes we were at the shore and we descended as quickly as possible to a nearby airport. The motor was sputtering as we hit the ground. Here are a few of these aerial shots.

"Golden Heritage, Golden Harvest"
Produced & Directed by Sumner Jules Glimcher
http://youtu.be/LzoqfmTcsxo

Now Their Home Is Israel

Since I love travel and have been blessed by knowing a few fascinating individuals, one of whom was Harold Flender, because this assignment encompassed both, it was one of my favorite projects. Here is how it all began.

Harold, whom you met in the Chapter when he and I made "North From Mexico," marched into my office at CMC one day and told me that he had a new assignment and wanted me to work with him. He had been asked by Hadassah to make a documentary in Israel on a program called, 'Youth Aliyah.' Since I was a non-practicing Jew, I knew little about Israel and had never been there. But my sympathies were with this small nation where, in contrast to Jewish behavior in World War II, the five or so million early settlers of this tiny slice of land, surrounded by one hundred million Arabs, fought ferociously to create and defend their new homeland. So naturally I was interested in knowing what Harold had to say.

After Hitler took power in January 1933, it became clear that German Jews were endangered, and in March 1936 German schools were closed to Jewish children. Reicha Freier, a rabbi's wife founded Youth Aliyah to protect German Jewish children by sending them to pioneer training programs in Palestine after completing elementary school.

But at first, Palestine had no way for absorbing these kids, typically six to sixteen years of age into its nascent society. Eddie Cantor, the American actor-comedian, gave a check for $25,000 to Hadassah, a social network of women and part of The Jewish Agency to fund this new program. They created a program and called it "Youth Aliyah" (the word 'Aliyah' in Hebrew means to 'fly up.') Hadassah established a series of kibbutz-like settlements scattered around Palestine headed by adults who acted "in loco parentis" to these parentless children who required mothers and fathers to guide these children into adulthood.

The children came not only from Germany, but also from other countries all around the world where anti-Semitism prospered. In 1971, Hadassah, headed by a far-sighted woman named Mamie Gameron, decided that her organization should sponsor a film to show this program, and asked Harold to create the program. Harold, who had apparently had such a happy experience working with me during North From Mexico, asked if CMC would sign the contract with Hadassah and if I would direct and produce this film! How could I not???

It was early December when we set our timetable: we would spend the month of January on location scouting many Youth Aliyah camps seeking youngsters to interview, then spend February working on the script, March shooting it, and April and May editing it. In mid-June, when Hadassah had its Annual luncheon in the Grand Ballroom of the Waldorf Astoria in New York, the film would have its premiere to an audience of 500. Our story would be based upon interviewing a variety of children whose lives had been saved by joining this new and remarkable group.

Harold and I agreed the essence of the film would be to find a wide variety of children, as diverse as we could find, and have them tell of their experiences, both at home where they grew up and had found hatred and discrimination, and then in Israel, where they became not only accepted, but also loved. And so this chapter will talk about how "interviews" can assume the story-telling role that makes all films of interest.

In the pre-production phase I talked with many friends who had made films in the Holy Land and gathered a variety of information that proved useful when we arrived. One friend, who had shot there on several occasions suggested that we avoid the King David Hotel, where most western visitors stayed, He suggested a small Arab-owned hotel in East Jerusalem called "The American Colony Hotel," where we would get the real flavor of the country and after acting on his suggestion, later blessed him for this suggestion.

Harold and I began our new adventure by boarding our El Al flight at JFK Airport, where we were exposed to the most thorough security examination I ever experienced. We were then put in First Class and enjoyed a most pleasant trip to the Israeli Airport, halfway between Tel Aviv and Jerusalem.

A representative of The Jewish Agency met us at the airport, and who, with his car and driver, told us that he would be pleased to take us to the King David Hotel. He seemed to be unnerved when we told him politely that we would be staying at 'The American Colony Hotel' in East Jerusalem, but took us there, nevertheless. As we drove through the oldest part of Jerusalem the architecture turned from the modern to that of a Cecil B. DeMille biblical extravaganza and the hotel itself was also biblical in its design. We entered and registered and the validity of it being a place for knowledgeable visitors was immediately made evident by running into two old NBC colleagues; Mary Ann Aschaffenburg, a producer of religious programs, and Marty Hoade, her director!

Prior to dropping us off, we had asked our Jewish Agency host if they might provide a car and driver for the next month. Having been instructed by New York to do whatever they could to make our trip productive, we were told that that would be arranged. We then arranged to dine with Mary Ann and Marty to get a first-hand briefing from two "Holy Land veterans."

One aspect that made collaboration between Harold and me special was that we both were early risers, and loved a pre-breakfast stroll through town each morning. There is little that could compare with a walk amidst the biblical architecture of East Jerusalem, and I took still images every time we turned another corner.

The native breakfast was also slightly unusual: a hard-cooked egg, flat bread and hummus, as well as coffee. Thus armed for the day we waited each morning for our car and driver. We immersed ourselves in the culture by visiting all the important local sites; the Dead Sea, Masada, the caves where the Dead Sea Scrolls had been discovered, and finally one of the Youth Aliyah villages near Jerusalem. There we met a thirteen-year-old girl named 'Zahava' (meaning 'gold' in Hebrew), who later became the backbone of our film. Unlike all the other interviewees in our film, Zahava was native-born, but had been selected to participate in Youth Aliyah because her family was dysfunctional and she could not study at home.

Her family lived in Haifa, and she left her Youth Aliyah village to visit home every three weeks, thus we decided to follow her on her trip to the north of the country, which gave us a device to stop off at various other Youth Aliyah villages along the way. In all we visited some nine Villages and ended up interviewing children from Peru, Iraq, Iran, Russia, Tunisia, Romania, South Africa, and France. As Harold and I met dozens of youngsters, our objective was to select bright, articulate kids who looked and acted differently to show the diversity of those who had been brought to Israel.

As we were winding down our month-long visit, Harold had an intriguing thought. He suggested that instead of returning to New York for the month of February to write the script, we go to Paris, instead! He said that Pairs would inspire him more than New York.

There was another good reason to spend a month in Paris: just before leaving New York, I had been asked by an editor at Simon & Schuster to write a textbook on filmmaking. In those early days when universities began teaching film, there were just two books used as texts. One was highly technical; the other highly artistic. S&S decided to commission a textbook somewhere in between. Since I was then teaching at Columbia University and was a Harvard alumnus, they had decided that I could be the writer to create a text that included both the technological and the artistic aspects of filmmaking!

Harold said that he knew a good inexpensive hotel on the left bank where we could get two rooms cheaply; he would work on the script each morning while I could work on my book; we would then meet for lunch, edit his script, and then enjoy Paris for the afternoon and evening!

There was even a third reason to select Paris as a stop. Since we had avoided fancy hotels and restaurants in Israel and had frequently been taken out for lunches and dinners, we had spent much less than I had budgeted for our scouting trip. Thus we could spend a month in Paris on the savings that had resulted.

We moved into the Hotel Madison on the left bank and the following month was a dream. The Hotel, in the heart of Saint Germaine-des-Pres, was once the home of Albert Camus, and Jean-Paul Sartre, and their spirits remained in its rooms. Each morning the hotel brought me a café au lait and a croissant for breakfast and I began to draft my book as I listened to my Bach music cassettes. By midday I would walk across the street to either Le Dome, Café Deux Magots, or Café Flore and Harold and I would enjoy a gourmet lunch while talking over the script. In the afternoon we would visit a museum or park, another gourmet meal for dinner and a movie or concert. Since Harold had lived in Paris previously, knew it inside out and was fluent in the language, this was one of the most pleasant months of my life. In his earlier stay there he had written "Paris Blues", later made into a movie featuring Paul Newman. But all good things come to an end and when the script was done, we packed up, flew back to New York, showed Hadassah the script and within a week had approval and were ready to return to shoot the film.

I asked Warren Johnson, my former student and talented Cinematographer to join me to shoot the images, knowing that I could hire a capable soundman in Israel. I had always wanted to see my wife, Joan, do some productive work, rather than just remain a housewife and a mother. I asked her to join our crew as the Production Manager. Warren, Joan and I along with several cases full of equipment, took off in early March to make the film. Arriving at the Israeli Airport, we knew exactly where we wanted to go and began work. Prior to having left on our scouting trip I had met and signed on a soundman and driver named Arye Rosenfield. I rented a large van, we packed all our gear into it, and headed to pick up our "star", Zahava, just outside Jerusalem, ready to go to go to work with us.

We drove directly to her home in Haifa, where we shot her saying goodbye to her family, then filmed her as she purchased her ticket on the first of the two bus trips (the first from Haifa to Tel Aviv, the second from Tel Aviv to Jerusalem). I plan to show you two interviews that we recorded on the trip back to Jerusalem. The first was when we interviewed two young girls: one was a slender soft-spoken young woman from South Africa; the other a flamboyant, robust young lady with wildly billowing hair from Paris.

"Now Their Home Is Israel"
Produced & Directed by Sumner Jules Glimcher
http://youtu.be/BbYndr9zrJc

The second interview was with two boys: one a fair, slender, articulate youngster from Russia; the other a swarthy young man from Iraq. These two interviews, I believe, show you a range of the differences among the kids selected to be brought to Israel.

"Now Their Home Is Israel"
Produced & Directed by Sumner Jules Glimcher
http://youtu.be/on652SjvIHs

The film concluded with a mass bar mitzvah at the Western Wall, just inside the Haifa Gate. As I was editing the final sequence it seemed to lack appropriate music. I hired a Westport Cantor, named Paul Kwartin to do a bit of liturgical music to enhance the closing.

The film was to have its premiere at the Hadassah Annual Luncheon in mid-June in the Grand Ballroom of the Waldorf Astoria in New York.

The room seated 500 and so we rented a high wattage projector situated on the balcony to a large screen on one side of the room. After the meal, the film was introduced by Ms. Gameron, the light dimmed and the half-hour film unspooled. At the end, there was thunderous applause. The ensuing year when the film was shown at various Hadassah meetings throughout the US, Hadassah was overwhelmed in donations. One lesson learned: you do not need to ask for money if your film demonstrates the need.

A Taste of Provence

This film, probably the most popular film I ever made, came about by accident. I never planned to make it.

I had just finished another assignment and happened to be flush with cash and badly needed a rest. My Harvard classmate and closest friend, Dick Kislik and his wife Audrey, decided at that time to sell their large country home on a lake in Westchester County, where I been a guest for many summer weekends. The absence of their four children, grown and gone, obviated their need for a very large summer place and Audrey no longer wanted the chore of the upkeep. As we sat on their deck contemplating the sale, Dick said the he was sorry that next year they would be unable to invite me on summer weekends, and, furthermore, he wasn't sure what he and Audrey would do as well.

On the spur of the moment I suggested that we all rent a villa in the south of France. I knew friends who had been doing that for many years in the past and loved it. My friend, Eric Arctander, a painter, and his wife went to a small farm in northern Provence for the month of May each year and recommended it highly. A few days later I had a call from Audrey saying that since she wanted to have her own kitchen, she decided that we should have separate places and she had found two next door apartments on the Cote d'Azure, had booked one, and gave me the information on the other.

I called my two eldest daughters who had frequently vacationed with me in the past and told them that I was thinking of renting a place in Southern France and if they had time and wanted to join me, would they prefer a farm in Northern Provence, or a villa on the Riviera?

Neither they said, you would hate either. The Riviera, near Nice and Cannes, will be jammed with rock stars and movie icons; the traffic will be horrendous, the restaurants expensive, and all the beaches filled with rocks. And a farm in a small town will be bereft of any social or cultural life and there will be nothing to do after sundown.

Since both Susan and Jennie had spent time in France and knew it much better than I, I paid attention to what they said. They suggested that Aix-en-Provence was the perfect town to visit. Aix was the cultural capital of Southern France and each July had a music festival. And then Jennie made me an offer I could not refuse; she said that she would look on the Internet and see if she might find the perfect villa. Thus in a week or so she forwarded the particulars of a villa in a town called "Bouc bel Air." It was in a small town on a hill 10km south of Aix and 20km north of Marseille. Her email said, "this is it!" and indeed it looked great! It had four bedrooms, two bathrooms, a small swimming pool a and a country kitchen perfect for cooking. It was available for the month of July that coming summer and the rental was $10,000 US. A bit steep, but the photos took my breath away. And so I booked it and sent a deposit.

Susan and Jennie flew from Dulles to de Gaulle International and I flew from LGA and we met in the French Airport on the first of July that following summer. Our flight to Marseille was delayed, but who cared? At Marseille I picked up our rental car, read once again the directions to our vacation villa and set off. Not surprising, we got lost so it was not until 10:00PM that we arrived at our new home. We were immediately cheered as we were met by the considerate realtor who had bought a rotisserie chicken to greet we hungry three.

The villa was better than we had expected; it was absolutely charming. After assuaging our hunger and getting briefed by the realtor we set off to our respective bedrooms and were quickly in dreamland.

The next morning we took a detailed tour of our new residence. I grabbed a quick morning swim and we checked out the fridge to find it fully stocked with eggs, bacon, juices, fruits and vegetables and made a big pot of coffee for an awesome breakfast. Now we were ready for four weeks of joyous adventures. It began with the short ten km trip to Aix where we parked and found a small cafe where we had our second breakfast; almond croissants and café au lait. Is there anything better than sitting in the morning sunshine with such a delicious repast at an outdoor table in a French café' watching the world pass by?

Not to be outdone by Jennie having found the villa, Susan brought along a file one inch thick of the research she had done on Provence; its places of interest; its artists, its towns, weather and historical treasures. Our first hour was spent as Susan read off some of the highlights she had found. Amongst the towns nearby, Avignon, Arles, Marseille, Cassis were just a short drive. The two artists who dominated Provence were Paul Cezanne and Vincent van Gogh, the writer, Victor Hugo (j'accuse!) had been born there and he grew up as best friends with Cezanne. My God, what a proliferation of history and art; where to begin? The next twenty-eight days were a whirlwind of food, wine, history, art, towns and villages. And music everywhere.

As noted, each July there was a music festival in Aix. In 2005 Mozart was being honored. Thus all the churches. concert halls, and even the streets were filled night and day with music ranging from 16th Century French liturgical motets to "Cosi fan Tutti." To go back to the beginning of this chapter, I had no intention of making a film, but it would have been ridiculous of me to spend a month abroad without my camera.

In the next four weeks our typical day would be, (after our morning Croissant and café, of course), to get on a local road, drive to a nearby destination, spend the day there, highlighted by a gourmet lunch and then hop onto one of the superhighways for a quick trip home. On the way home we always stopped for a visit to a farmer's market where we purchased fresh dinner ingredients and then come home to prepare our evening meal.

Usually one or the other girl would drive, the non-driver would navigate and tell us what we would be about to see, and I sat in the front seat next to the driver shooting video as we drove. Who ever heard of The Camargue before visiting? The Chateaus that defended the Western borders of Provence? How salt was harvested from the seas? And restaurants that served ten different varieties of Moules?

Susan and Jennie were able to take just two weeks off work and so they spent the first two weeks of July with me. Not wanting to waste the last two weeks alone in this magnificent villa I had earlier invited two close friends from the Harvard Club to spend the last two weeks sharing my villa. Sally and Peter Johnson had frequently spent summers in France and so they became my companions for the last two weeks of July. While I had been, more or less, the major chef for or evening dinners during our first two weeks, Peter also a great chef, and he and I shared cooking duties the last two weeks; he one night, I the next. Sally who loved to eat well did not mind the cleaning up afterwards, For our final dinner, I prepared a pan-roasted breast of duck, garlic mashed potatoes and salad. Peter prepared a chocolate soufflé. I recorded them as we toasted each other as the camera panned over the main course and that became the final shot in the film.

After returning home I viewed all the footage and was amazed to see how thoroughly I had had 'covered' our trip. After stripping away much of the repetitive or uninteresting footage, it seemed as if I had an hour of pretty interesting stuff. When I added the music, I ended up with an hour that I titled: *"A Taste of Provence: Art, History & Culture."*

When Aldon James, then the Executive Director of the National Arts Club on Gramercy Park in New York, first saw the film, he wrote me saying: "Dear Sumner, You are a genius and must join the National Arts Club."

He asked me to show the film, describe how I made it, and then end the evening with a duplicate of the Provencal dinner that ended the film. He charged members $70 for the evening and 150 people came for the event. A year later, he repeated the event and another 100 came. Two years later, once again another 100, so in total 350 people enjoyed seeing my film.

Here are a few excerpts:

"A Taste Of Provence: History, Art & Culture"
Produced & Directed by Sumner Jules Glimcher
http://youtu.be/F1Cipye3HJs

"A Taste Of Provence: History, Art & Culture"
Produced & Directed by Sumner Jules Glimcher
http://youtu.be/tbz2jaHgYz4

"A Taste Of Provence: History, Art & Culture"
Produced & Directed by Sumner Jules Glimcher
http://youtu.be/cCorhaOoeco

"A Taste Of Provence: History, Art & Culture"
Produced & Directed by Sumner Jules Glimcher
http://youtu.be/mJUlXFqwHVc

If you enjoyed what you saw, you may download the entire film onto your computer. Visit the link below for more details.

http://www.sumnerjulesglimcher.com/Official/Videos.html

Masterpieces of Chinese Art

As a frequent visitor to China and Japan, I had always enjoyed the very different art of both countries; in a simplification that of the woodblock art of Japan, with Ando Hiroshige as it's foremost practitioner, and the grand eloquence of Chinese art with its focus on nature and showing man as an insignificant speck in the huge Chinese landscape scrolls favored by Chinese landscape artists. So when asked by Gene Loh (see chapter Seven on *"Golden Heritage, Golden Harvest"*) to make his film on Taiwan, I wondered if, perhaps, I might take this opportunity to film The National Palace Museum in Taipei?

For those who do not know the history and politics of the Mao tse-tung conquest of China, here is an important footnote having to do with how Communism affected Chinese art.

When Mao banished Chiang Kai-shek from the Chinese mainland in 1949, Chiang took with him every piece of Chinese art that was not nailed down. That included not only scrolls of paintings, ivory, and lacquer, but also fragile Ming jade, calligraphy, sculpture, superb Tang ivory horses, porcelain and the early bronzes of the Shang Dynasty. In essence the only art he left behind was the actual architecture of the Forbidden Palace itself.

Once established in Taipei, he built what he called "The National Palace Museum" and stocked it with all the treasure he had brought with him from the mainland. He said he was protecting the heritage of Chinese art from the barbarians, who in turn, accused him of looting China's artistic heritage. After witnessing Mao's Cultural Revolution, the answer is not so easily answered. Nevertheless, there sat the essence of Chinese art in the National Palace Museum, unseen except by those fortunate enough to visit Taipei.

I told Harold Mason, my partner, of my thoughts when Loh offered us a contract to produced the documentary he wanted made on Taiwan. I suggested that we ask Mr. Loh for a two-film contract, and Harold agreed, provided that we did not endanger his initial offer. Much to our joy, Loh send our message to Taipei, and in a few days the answer came back: Taiwan would agree to both films and pay for both!

Since I knew nothing about Chinese history, dynasties or art, how would I know what to film? I asked friends far more knowledgeable about Chinese art than I and was given an important name: i.e. that of Tom Lawton at the Freer Gallery of Art in Washington, D.C. Lawton had taken his PhD in Chinese Art and written his dissertation at the National Palace Museum! Here was the expert I needed. I wrote him and asked if he would help and of course he said he would be delighted.

Once again I persuaded my wife that she should try her hand as a writer and suggested that she be the writer of the film on Chinese Masterpieces. She agreed and joined me on my first and subsequent visits with Lawton. Joan and I spent valuable time with Lawton in Washington with our tape recorder before going on location and he gave us a few stills that portrayed significant holdings in the museum. The final script that she later wrote is one of the finest pieces of work that is part of my entire filmography; it is a masterpiece of scriptwriting!

Lawton was the perfect consultant: exceedingly knowledgeable, very cooperative and clearly expert on every aspect of the Museum's holdings. We estimated how many hours of his time I would need, agreed on a fee and then began to work. We spent four hours with him recording his every word on tape, and as a bonus, in describing some specific objects he drew on many of his books and copied page after page of certain objects. One example was a copy he made of one of several lacquer plates, so that I would find the right one while on location. This was enormously helpful, as I found out later on location, as I learned that his knowledge of the Museum's holdings was far more accurate that that of the local curators, who truly knew far less! Now armed with a great list of what to film, from Shang bronzes of pre-history, to the Tang Horses, Ming porcelain and Sung scrolls by such experts as Fan Kwan, Gua Hsi and Jiao Guan, I was prepared to go to work on 'Masterpieces.'

After we had completed photography on what we later called *"Golden Heritage Golden Harvest,"* we learned that we had been granted three days in the photography room of the Museum. I met the Director of the Museum, a man named Chiang fu-tsung, and learned to my delight that his only foreign language was German, the language I was most familiar with, so we hit it off immediately when he and a group of his curators invited Joan, Warren and me to a spectacular Chinese banquet.

Another bit of information. When Chiang kai-shek was deported from the Chinese mainland, he took with him all the rich people and the rich all took their chefs, so the finest Chinese cuisine in the world is now on Taiwan. As one who adores Chinese food I have dined in world-renowned cities such as New York, San Francisco, Los Angeles, London, Paris and many other cities, but never have I experienced more authentic and divine Chinese food than in Taiwan!

In our three days if shooting in the Museum, our greatest difficulties were the curators who, when they displayed their fragile Chinese scrolls, never allowed us more than thirty seconds of light before turning the lights off. And they handled the ju-ware as the precious jewels that they undoubtedly were.

When we finished shooting, I knew it was my turn to invite Chiang and his staff to a Chinese banquet that I would host. We were staying at the Grand Palace Hotel, the incredible pavilion that had been designed by Madame Chiang. For those of you who have seen the film, "Eat, Drink, Man, Woman" the kitchen portrayed in that film was that of the Grand. Ang Lee, the Taipei native who, later went to the NYU Film School, directed this film. Thus, when I told the chef at the Grand that my guest of honor at the banquet would be the Director of the National Palace Museum (in China, art and age are far more honored than in our country), the chef provided us with a feast unlike any other I had ever experienced. Between the cuisine, the culture of the society, and the work we were doing, this was another month full of joy. Here is one sequence from "Masterpieces." Among my favorites were the Shang bronzes.

"Masterpieces Of Chinese Art"
Produced & Directed by Sumner Jules Glimcher
http://youtu.be/kBcu8jeWwIA

Old World, New Women

The first two films we made for Taiwan "Golden Heritage, Golden Harvest" & "Masterpieces of Chinese art" were both translated into seven languages and shown in diplomatic circles all around the world. The government was so pleased by their reception that two years later, as the women's movement was recognized by several of the more forward nations in the world, Taiwan invited me to return to make a film about how Chinese women had been treated. And they took advantage of what they had learned in the first instance: i.e. having me make a second film while I was there. After determining that the principal project would have the subject of "the role of the woman in Chinese society" they gave me the option of choosing the subject of the second film on my own. It did not take me long to choose the subject to be "Confucius" which absolutely delighted my hosts. Working on my knowledge that choosing him as my subject would allow me to learn far more about an individual whom I had long admired, indeed making this film taught me much about this incredible person. I shall share what I learned about him in the next chapter.

Once again I asked Warren Johnson to be my cinematographer and my wife Joan, in this instance, to be the writer, and the three of us flew to Taipei to spend a full month on location. When we arrived, the Foreign Office assigned a driver/interpreter to the project and he had a long list of women prominent in a variety of professions.

One of the first women we met was a teacher of English and she was so fluent and obviously sharp that we decided to make her our narrator and she became the glue that held the film together. We see her first in the classroom with an all female class as she calls upon several of her students to read aloud. Then she introduces us to a novelist who tells us that she wrote, neither for fame nor money, but because she felt that everyone should be useful. She had time on her hands and began to write, and now has six novels under her belt.

We segued from the novelist to an utterly charming television director whom we see at first talking with a male and female dual vocalists on the set and then in the control room as she directs the cameras. From this light TV fare we go next to a serious period costume drama and in this control room we meet Chen Su-ming. Su-ming was graduated from Louvain

University in Belgium, returned to her home in Taipei, and twenty-five years later had become the head of Taiwan TV!

Continuing in the field of communications we discover a colorful woman, who started a newspaper in Taipei. Her husband an individual who new how to improvise, collected old batteries and melted the lead down to create letters for their linotype machine which printed out the first newspaper in Taiwan. At first a History major in college she tells us that her husband explained to her that journalism was the history of tomorrow.

Other accomplished women included a judge in the Legislative body, who also taught law at Tai da (the local nickname for National Taiwan University); a Confucian scholar who tells us that Confucius saw women as the center of the family, thus the most important person in the family who trained the leaders of the future. Swallow Lin, a wood block artist and the Cloud-Gate Ensemble, a modern dance group who performed for our film.

We also interviewed a computer systems analyst, an architect and a surgeon. One special note: Warren, who had no taste for blood, became nauseous when the surgeon made her first incision and had to leave the room. He turned the camera over to me when the blood began to flow leaving me to shoot the operation by myself.

Here is a sequence from "Old World, New Women," showing a female director of a feature film.

"Old World, New Women"
Produced & Directed by Sumner Jules Glimcher
http://youtu.be/0eQwJA2o04U

Confucius

The question was: how do you make a film about a guy who has been dead for 2,500 years? The answer was, if he was famous and left some of his writings: it was not too hard. The first thing I did was to read whatever I could about him, and if you go to Google, you will find out there is quite a lot. In fact, eleven full single-spaced pages. When one considers history, there is probably no single individual who has played a more important role involving more people than Confucius.

He was born (551-479BC) in the Province of Lu during the Spring and Autumn period of Chinese history. He was a teacher, editor, scholar, politician and philosopher. One of the most striking elements of his life is that Socrates (born in 469 BC in Greece), and Gautama Buddha (born in 563 BC in India) and Aristotle (born in 384 BC, also in Greece), as well as Confucius, four of the most important sages, all born in vastly different parts of the world, were all born during a finite period of time. Might it simply be coincidence, or was there something in the air?

In any event, because of his philosophy and his emphasis in personal and governmental morality and his correctness of social relationships, justice and sincerity, he was highly thought of during his lifetime. His Five Classics and his Analects lived on after his death. He championed strong family loyalty, ancestor worship, respect of elders by their children, and of husbands by their wives. He espoused the well-known principle "Do not do to others what you do not want done to yourself," an early version of the Golden Rule.

In the Wade-Giles system of Romanization his name is rendered as 'Kung Fu-tzu,' literally 'Kung, the Master.' In modern times there were two significant differences in The People's Republic of China and in Taiwan and how they treated Confucius. On the mainland the Communists in their clumsy attempt to discard all 'old ways' of China attempted to disown Kung during the Cultural Revolution and for some four decades the Communists declared him persona non grata. But the people would have none of that and secretly he remained their sage. In Taiwan, on the other hand, he never lost his glory. His birthday, September 28th, a ceremony instigated during the Ming Dynasty, was celebrated without interruption in Taiwan. And so we began our film by shooting the annual celebrations, made somewhat difficult by the fact that it began pre-dawn! Once, when asked if there might be one word to guide one through life he suggested "reciprocity."

The Confucian theory of ethics is exemplified by the Chinese word, "li." Li is based upon three important conceptualized aspects of life: Ceremonies associated with sacrifice to ancestors and other deities; social and political institutions; and the etiquette of daily behavior. In Confucianism, "Li" is closely associated with "Yi," which is based upon reciprocity. Thus an outcome of yi is doing the right thing for the right reason. Yi is closely linked to ren. Ren consists of five basic virtues: seriousness, generosity, sincerity, diligence and kindness.

Thus armed with this most basic knowledge, Joan (writer); Warren (cinematographer/editor); and I (producer/director) took flight to Taiwan. On this occasion, we had been hired to make two films: the role of women in Chinese society (see previous chapter) and Confucius, much dearer to my heart. In terms of timing we had to be in Taipei before September 28th.

The ceremony, which began well before dawn, was dimly lit, mostly by candlelight. With music, most of which was dramatic drums, both Warren and I prayed that we would get usable images on the film we had brought along; the fastest ASA rating Kodak had at that time. The stage was slowly filled with hundreds of acolytes all clad in white.

The ceremony dramatically progressed as the costumed performers climbed to the stage. As dawn approached, we saw tinges of blue and orange color the sky. We shot every minute of the ceremony and luckily we did, as the ceremony became the backbone of the film.

Afterwards we interviewed two Confucian scholars; one male the other female who spoke of Confucius in their native Mandarin, all of which was then translated on the spot by our elegant female interpreter. Each in their own words, confirmed the essence of what I had learned earlier.

One more short interview was with the 77th lineal descendent of Confucius, who introduced his daughter and two grandchildren. He spoke in Mandarin, his daughter in English.

While I knew that the actual ceremony would be the spine of the film, I knew that we would also require additional footage so I found scrolls and screens of images that I believed might illustrate much of what I knew would be in the final script, in the National Palace Museum. I also recorded a Koto player who played a variety of short, pithy chords and passages. As we pieced together what I felt we would need, Joan was working on the script. She and I had early begun to think of the script as a dialogue between two individuals: one, the narrator; the other Confucius himself.

For several reasons, chief among them being, that Confucius influenced so many people, was that he lived in the most populous nation extant. Thus his ideas naturally were heard and followed by hundreds of millions of Chinese.

"Confucius"
Produced & Directed by Sumner Jules Glimcher
http://youtu.be/pfusTQGRDho

"Confucius"
Produced & Directed by Sumner Jules Glimcher
http://youtu.be/LdpKU5JmZXo

Memento

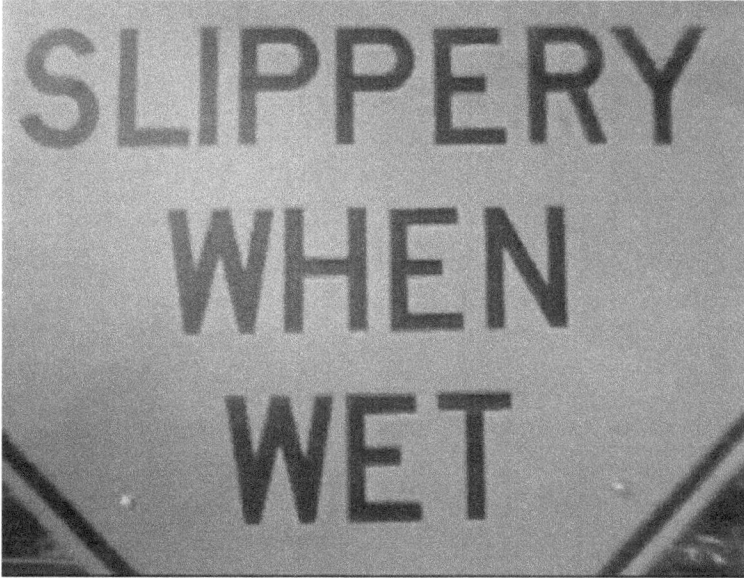

I was in Washington, D.C. at a dinner where recipients were receiving awards for their films and sitting next to Bill Pratt, the person at AT&T who was responsible for the films sponsored by AT&T. He mentioned to me that AT&T, which at that time had 900 employees, lost an inordinate amount of time by employees who left work for sick time. Most of this sick time was due to automobile accidents and he wondered what kind of film might be made of to lessen auto accidents? I have probably written earlier how much of my life and career has been driven by accident. The film in this chapter, "Memento" is a prefect example of this connection.

At that time I was the Manager of the Center for Mass Communication (CMC) at Columbia University, and my colleague, Erik Barnouw had scribbled out a two-page memo on a film on auto accidents. Erik, who had built a tiny one-room vacation house in Vermont, as he drove north on summer weekends, had noticed a number of 'automobile graveyards.' In particular he was aware that not only did these 'graveyards' house old and rusted hulks, but many also had brand new automobiles, which had been crushed in recent accidents. That sparked his always-active imagination and he came up with an idea that caused this film to be made. So when Pratt said that to me. I told him that perhaps CMC might be able to help, and that I would send him a proposal when I returned to New York.

Erik had titled his suggested film, "Memento" and his concept was as follows. It would be a very short film; just nine minutes and would consist of three, three-minute sequences. In each of these sequences, an automobile accident would occur. Each accident was caused by a different event, and at the end of each sequence we would see the damaged vehicle in the junkyard. In each sequence, in addition to the visuals the sound tracks would be a crucial element.

In the first sequence a man and wife are driving. He is speeding and his wife asks him to slow down. He does not and hits a car at an intersection, We see a series of quick cuts of broken glass In the second sequence we see the flashing of ambulance red lights. We hear the voices of a policeman and the young girl who was driving and she is upset and weeping. Apparently a young guy was driving alongside, but not passing since he was trying to chat her up. They come to a curve and he doesn't make it and presumably was killed.

The third sequence is the most dramatic. A guy is driving, his wife in the passenger seat and their young child is in the back seat. It is pouring rain and the visibility is very poor. We are looking through the windshield, the windshield wipers going back and forth. We see flash frames of "SPEED LIMIT 45 MPH" and "SLIPPERY WHEN WET." As they come to an intersection, we hear the wife calling, "TOM, TOM" and the child screaming, "DADDY, DADDY," then the sound the crash, then utter silence as we have a series of quick cuts of broken glass. Every time I play this sequence, it hits a raw nerve.

When I sent Pratt the proposal, he called me back immediately, loved the concept and commissioned the project within 24 hours. When the film was completed, AT&T loved it, ordered us to make 200 35mm prints, which they handed out to theaters across the country to play as a Public Service. This film won more major national and international awards, than any other film I ever made. Here is the final sequence.

"Memento"
Executive Producer Sumner Jules Glimcher
http://youtu.be/XBfK45B_IEA

September, 2001: A Personal Memoir

Once again, accidental timing, this time on a monumental level, caused the production of a documentary of a historic nature. Early one morning, I had been swimming in the pool in the Coles NYU Gym at Bleecker Street. When I emerged into the lobby, there on a television monitor, I saw the two twin Towers at the World Trade Center downtown were on fire. I crossed the street to my number One Washington Square Village Building walked into my apartment, grabbed my video camera, my tripod and a couple of tapes and went downstairs to the corner of Bleecker Streets and LaGuardia Place, which had an unobstructed view downtown.

I opened my tripod, put a tape into the camera, set it onto the tripod, and pointed it downtown. Although the World Trade Center was a mile and a half away, I zoomed to a close-up and started the camera at 10:00AM. At one minute past 10:00 the South Tower collapsed in a cloud of dust and I had a close-up of it on tape! As mentioned earlier, I had had my basic training in the first six years of my career at NBC, and part of that had been working at NBC NEWS. I ran upstairs, called NBC NEWS, told them what I had and they said to bring it in immediately. Downstairs all the subways had been locked down, but I secured a ride in a passing private car uptown on Sixth Avenue to 49th Street, where I had a hard time persuading the guards at Rock Center to allow me into the building.

I finally made it to the WNBC local newsroom, which, although in a state of panic seized my tape, screened it and immediately put it on the air. They then sent me to the NETWORK NEWSROOM, but there was nobody there. I left them a note and went back downtown. By morning the wind had shifted and the acrid smell of the burning buildings was so pervasive and unpleasant that I decided to leave NY for my Vermont ski house, where the air was as pure as it gets. A couple of days later, sitting on my sun-splashed deck my telephone rang. It was the NBC NETWORK, which had somehow tracked me down, who wanted to purchase international rights, I negotiated with them over the phone, sold them all rights and told them I would sign an agreement when I returned to New York.

I drove back to New York a few days later and decided to create a documentary of the event. Aside from the actual attack, it seemed to me that a record of the event, including the clean up, might be useful. And so I took my camera and walked south to where the twin towers had been. There was a huge Press Area where TV crews from all around the world were recording whatever they could find pertinent to the attack. The cleaning up of the debris was the predominant activity and squads of trucks, police, firemen and mountains of steel from the towers were being hauled away. It was an eerie and surreal scene and I spent several days recording it all. Once the area was cleared, I took my footage and created the film: "September, 2011: A Personal Memoir." Here are a few scenes.

"September 2001: A Personal Memior"
Produced & Directed by Sumner Jules Glimcher
http://youtu.be/LERgPUW8SqA

"September 2001: A Personal Memior"
Produced & Interviewed by Sumner Jules Glimcher
http://youtu.be/w4i59O21Ng8

In The Shadow Of The Vampire

Michael Servetus, who was burned at the stake in 1553 for his theological treatise "On the Errors of the Trinity," was generally considered as the first person whose 'anti-trinitarian' views as the Unitarian Pioneer and first Martyr. The Protestant Reformation, occurring about the same time, professed a large degree of tolerance, and a repugnance to established dogma. Hungary and Transylvania were places where early Unitarianism flourished. In recent times, Transylvanian Unitarians were suffering discriminating practices, by the ruling regimes. Thus, in 1989, the Unitarian/ Universalist Headquarters in Boston had asked American 'UUs' to each 'adopt' a Transylvanian church and help it as a 'sister' church.

Since I had found the Unitarian dogma, or really the lack of it, far more tolerant of spiritualism than my birth religion of Judaism, I found myself attending the Unitarian Church of Westport, CT, as a more or less spiritual home. Most especially, since a minister named Frank Hall had spent the past 29 years presenting weekly sermons that gave me a spiritual lift each Sunday. Our Westport church adopted a church in a tiny town in Transylvania, which since WWII is now a part of Romania, In July of 2004, one of our parishioners named Jo Shute decided to lead a group from Westport to visit our sister church in "Alsoboldogfalva."

In all, there were ten of us who flew to the Bucharest Airport, then boarded a large van for the four-hour drive over the Carpathian Mountains to the tiny village of some 800 souls. Among our group was an extraordinary person named Sally Swing Shelley. Sally was one of the children of Raymond Gram Swing, an early radio broadcasting pioneer and contemporary of Lowell Thomas. Raymond, to show his support for feminism, when he married Betty Gram, an ardent feminist, took his wife's last name as his middle name; a notable act around the early part of the last century. I had met Sally and her husband, Jim Shelley, neighbors in Easton, who occasionally attended the Unitarian Church in Westport, and, kindred spirits, we quickly became close friends.

At that time Sally worked at the Department of Public Information in the United Nations, and one of her responsibilities was producing a radio interview show, which was widely distributed across the United States. Each week she would interview a significant figure; usually a person deeply involved in international political affairs. One of the things that drew us together was that, from time to time, when Sally traveled on UN business, she asked me to fill in for her as host of the show.

When we met, she was putting together a book consisting of a series of love letters she had received from a particularly interesting fellow with whom she had had an earlier love affair; Jean-Paul Sartre. When she was graduated from Smith College, around 1950, her dad, then stationed in Paris, invited her there to join him. There she met Sartre, instantly fell in love with him, and was the happy recipient of some 80-love letters over the two-year affair. Since we shared literary passions, she asked me to read and comment on the letters, which by then had been translated into English, which I did with keen interest. And so, when I decided to join the group going to Transylvania, and mentioned it to her, she quickly decided to come along, realizing that this trip would provide her with some actual international fodder for her radio series.

Since she and I stood out among the group…she with her tape recorder, and me with my video camera, for I had decided to record the trip… she and I were housed at the residence of the minister of their tiny local Unitarian church. His name was Biro Mihaly; Biro, his family name was pronounced first and then Mihaly (pronounced MEE HI), pronounced second. One of the elements of the trip was that each of us stayed with a local family, thus saving hotel and restaurant expenses. We arrived as dusk was falling, given a quick supper and fell into bed.

Awakened at dawn by the crowing of roosters, looking out the window I saw a cow across the dirt road heading out to join the herd of fifty local cows headed out to pasture for the day. After breakfast, Sally and I, accompanied by Mihaly and a young girl named Sofi, who was our interpreter, headed into town to interview a few inhabitants.   First there were two elderly men; Janos and Danesh, respectively 81 and 79. Their weather-beaten faces testified to a lifetime as farmers and they spoke of their youth, their disdain of most television, except for the Hungarian-speaking Channel, and their contentment in their simple lives.

"In The Shadow Of The Vampire"
Produced & Directed by Sumner Jules Glimcher
http://youtu.be/3Xg5NEqDxDE
We went into the fields to see the farmers at work and stopped first to talk with a father and son who were raking hay.

"In The Shadow Of The Vampire"
Produced & Directed by Sumner Jules Glimcher
http://youtu.be/fXNmHQ_W9bQ

On our second day, Jo had arranged a van to take us to a few nearby places. Our first visit was to Szekely Keresztur where we visited the Molnar Museum, named for Istvan Molnar, where early agricultural tools had been preserved. From there we drove to Szekely Udvarhey, where we found an enormous

Unitarian Church whose pastor, Russ Domokus told us that his congregation, drawn from all the small towns surrounding this hub city, numbered over 2,000 parishioners! Imagine!

Our last stop of the day was to visit a woman named Eva Kellerman, who with her husband, Levente had founded a dairy. Her town in Transylvania was named Okland, whose US partner church was that based in Oakland, California had provided over $200,000 US dollars which enabled Eva and Levente to create a farm which housed dozens of heifers which were lent out to poor Okland families to provide milk, butter and cheese. In addition to running the dairy, Eva was the coordinator of visiting US UUs, and in her day job was the principal of the local nursery. Levente was the pastor of their local church.

"In The Shadow Of The Vampire"
Produced & Directed by Sumner Jules Glimcher
http://youtu.be/m5HhdOQzXOk
We had a highly unusual interview with the daughter of one of our interpreters, Gisike. She had a four-year-old daughter names Agnes, one of the most precocious kids I had ever met. Agnes, who was learning English from her mom, spoke modest English and demonstrated her proficiency in the language as we spoke. Her charm dominated our talk.

"In The Shadow Of The Vampire"
Produced & Directed by Sumner Jules Glimcher

http://youtu.be/OwuWrQryamQ

The next few days were spent in towns and in the fields interviewing farmers making hay, tending their crops, and shepherds tending their flocks. Their simple basic lives were reminiscent of life in America one or two hundred years ago; free of our present city lives filled with automobiles, traffic, and what we call 'civilization.' However before we departed we took one more field trip.

On our second trip we visited the medieval town of Segeschvar and then Bertholem Castle. Segeschvar was known for two important historical elements: a huge clock tower in the center of town, and the birthplace of Vlad Tepes, later known as Vlad, the Impaler. We drove through the town up a series of hills to Bertholem Castle, the seat of the Roman Bishops, built in the 14th Century. It's interior was dominated by a huge painting of Jesus on the Cross-and an enormous organ. It also had a large Treasure Room, which had a heavy door that could be secured by a series of intricate locks and dead bolts.

Then we returned to Segeshvar where we saw the birthplace of Vlad Tepes born in 1431. His father was Vlad Dracul, which meant 'Vlad, The Dragon.' The son took the name Dracul-a, which meant 'Son of the Dragon.' When he became the ruler of Wallachia, the local district, his passion was impaling his enemies. When Mehmet The Conqueror invaded Wallachia he came across a high meadow on which he saw twenty thousand impaled bodies. Mehmet was so distraught that he felt he could not continue his advance and left the field of battle. In 1981 when Bram Stoker, a Scottish writer, invented Vampires, his model was said to be that of Vlad, The Impaler.

To return to a more peaceful element, upon our return to Alsoboldogfalva we visited the only factory in town. It was a furniture factory headed by Istvan, the father of our interpreter, Gisike, and the grandfather of little four–year old Agnes.

On our very last visit, we drove to a nearby gypsy village where the inhabitants had constructed a wooden platform on a nearby hillside so that they could put on a native dance. A Master Fiddler, and his fellow musicians, appeared along with a group of men and women, all festively attired, and we watched as they performed.

John Kaichrio Inadomi

"We Won't Come Out Alive"

Many years ago I was retained by a young Japanese man who, after we worked together became a close friend. His name was Ken Inadomi, and he asked me to create what I call a "Video Portrait" of his grandfather: John Kaichiro Inadomi. It was in 1998 and it was the one hundredth anniversary of JK's birth. It was the typical American success story, but from an oriental point of view.

JK was born into an impoverished family in Japan, scrimped and saved and came to America as a penniless 16-year-old boy and got a job in a lemon grove in California. After several years of savings he purchased a small store in a nearby town. When he had earned enough money, he returned to Japan, found a wife and brought her back to America. His business thrived and he built a second store but along came Word War

II and all Japanese, living on the west coast, loyal to America or not, were interned in one of the most disgraceful acts this country ever did. JK lost his businesses, his home, and his livelihood, as well.

When the war was over, he returned to where he had lived, borrowed money on his life insurance policy, and rebuilt his home and one new store. Again his hard work enabled his business to thrive, and by the time of his retirement and later death, he owned six large stores in southern California that in total was grossing sixty million dollars a year! His family had also flourished and he and his wife had had six children, Ken, a strapping thirty–year-old, one of his grandsons, was married with a small daughter, and commissioned me to create a 'portrait' of his granddad. It was an honor for me to work with Ken and together we created: "John Kaichiro Inadomi: A Centennial Celebration." Since JK was many years ago departed, the problem was how to tell his story.

Of his six children, five were still alive, so I decided that an interview with these remaining children telling stories about their dad should be the spine of the program. In fact the memories of these five provided a wonderful picture of the old man in itself. Their stories were colorful and were told with droll humor and obvious love. In addition to these five individuals, I also interviewed Ken's two brothers. Thus we had five children and two grandchildren. I also discovered a Japanese historian who provided a bit of historical data on the family background.

We then had a massive amount of interviews and went on a search for images to augment the words. Some were found in family archives; some were discovered on the Internet.

Ken then sat with me in an editing room, helping provide continuity. Although his modesty prevented him from being seen on camera, his narration, also recorded with love and passion, gave the film a most personal feeling. Here we see the US Military as they rounded up the internees.

"John Kaichiro Inadomi: A Celebration"
Produced & Directed by Sumner Jules Glimcher
http://youtu.be/5 ttIiyJrN0

The Panama Canal: History & Operation

I made this film as a result of one of the most interesting aspects of my life: that of being a luxury cruise ship lecturer. About the time that I retired from teaching at NYU, in the spring of 1988, I had a phone call from a woman who said that she booked luxury line cruise ship lecturers, and one of her lecturers had cancelled and she needed somebody who could show pictures and talk about China. She had heard that I gave slide lectures on China and Japan. She told me that the person who had cancelled was Harrison Salisbury the NEW YORK TIMES expert on Communism, especially expert on the USSR and CHINA. I told her that I could not fill his shoes.

Nevertheless she was insistent and told me that she needed someone to talk on the "Sea Princess." I asked her when it would be sailing and she responded in two weeks. I told her that I could not go on such short notice, but perhaps another time.

I called my three daughters and told them that I had been asked to speak on the "Sea Princess" but could not do so in two weeks. My kids responded in shock, telling me that the 'Sea Princess' was "The Love Boat." Since I did not watch much television, of course I had no idea what "The Love Boat" was.

Sure enough, she called again asking if I could go in the fall. Of course I accepted and thus began a series of cruise lectures on eleven different cruise liners. On one occasion, I transited the Panama Canal and ended up in Alaska. I always shot video on these trips.

Soon after returning I visited my friend, Sam Streeter, the contractor who helped me build my ski house in Vermont. When I mentioned this transit, this 'country boy' who was far more literate than I, asked me if I had ever read "The Path Between the Seas" by David McCullough. Of course I had not, but after reading it, I was so enthused that I quickly boarded a Washington Metroliner and spent the next month at the Library of Congress researching still images shot by the photographers sent to Panama by Teddy Roosevelt during the decade-long construction. What an amazing story I uncovered!

As early as during the presidency of Ulysses S. Grant, the United States had been interested in the possibilities of a canal traversing the Isthmus of Panama. During his time in office several times US Naval ships were dispatched to survey the Isthmus. In the 1800s, there were three ways to get from either one of the two oceans that encapsulated the United Sates: overland across the US frontier; by sea around the Cape of Good Horn at the southern tip of South America; or through the jungle in Central America), none were entirely practical.

The discovery of gold in California in 1849 sparked an enormous new interest in getting from the East Coast to the West; safely and rapidly. Eventually a railroad was constructed across the isthmus in 1855. However it was clear that an all-water route was the ideal solution. The Industrial Revolution, which brought new and vastly more efficient equipment, such as huge steam shovels and giant dredges, to bear on this new venture, made a canal a real possibility.

Meanwhile events in Europe occurred with eventual ramifications to a canal in Central American. The Suez Canal, a sea level canal; (i.e. one without locks), had been constructed, under the supervision of a Frenchman named Ferdinand de Lessups. De Lessups, a force of nature, decided that he would have a go at building a canal across the Central American isthmus. This man, whose first wife had died after giving him six sons, at age 65, remarried a 20-year-old farm girl who bore him twelve more children!

In 1883 De Lessups raised vast sums of money in France and began the first real effort to build the canal. However, due to accidents and disease (malaria and yellow fever) more than 22,000 workers died. The men in charge had little knowledge of engineering. Cuts through mountains had to be continually widened due to landslides, and after a six-year attempt to tame the jungle, he quit. The towns and villages he built were abandoned, as was all the machinery he had brought to Panama. The enormous financial loss (some $287,000,000USD), this ill-fated disaster caused, came close to bankrupting the French Empire. De Lessups spent his last years in disgrace.

Meanwhile in America, Teddy Roosevelt, who became widely know as a result of his charge in the Battle of San Juan Hill during the Mexican-American War, had been put on the ticket as vice-president when William McKinley was elected President. Thus becoming President after the McKinley assassination, Teddy was seeking dragons to slay. The situation in Central American intrigued him.

Panama was then a province of Colombia, and Secretary John Hayes had written a treaty with Dr. Tomas Herrain of Colombia, granting a renewable lease in perpetuity on the land proposed for the canal. In Bogota, the Colombians delayed in signing this treaty, saying that it favored the US more than Colombia. Philippe Bunau-Varilla, Chief Engineer and significant shareholder of the French canal company, told Hayes and Roosevelt of a possible revolution by Panamanian rebels who plotted to revolt against Colombia.

In fact, in November 1903 the rebellion occurred in Panama City, and Roosevelt sent US warships to the coast of Panama to prevent Colombian troops from putting down the rebellion. This spawned the term "gunboat diplomacy." Thus the US, by quickly recognizing the new nation, in spite of its largely deplored military actions, signed a treaty far more favorable to itself rather than to Bogota. For many decades this wound festered until President Jimmy Carter returned ownership of the Canal to Panama in a treaty dated in 1977 that took effect in 1999.

The US formally took control of the land on which this new Canal would be built on May 4, 1904, inheriting a vast jumble of buildings and equipment. A US government commission, the Isthmian Canal Commission (ICC), was established to oversee construction. The ICC reported directly to Secretary of War, William Howard Taft. The US paid the French government $40 million USD for all equipment, buildings and the Panama Railroad. The US also paid the new government of Panama $10 million USD plus $250,000 per year

Colonel William C. Gorgas was immediately appointed as Chief Sanitation Officer with a mandate to wipe disease off the map. Gorgas, aware that mosquitoes were the source of infectious malaria and yellow fever, instantly initiated measures to stop the spreading of these diseases. He sprayed insect-breeding areas with oil, put mosquito-stopping netting on all windows and eliminated all standing water. It took just a short time to entirely eliminate all disease from the Canal Zone.

John Frank Wallace was appointed as the first Chief Engineer at the same time Gorgas was appointed as Chief of Sanitation. Overwhelmed by the disease-plagued community and dilapidated French equipment, he quit after one year. John Frank Stevens, a self-educated engineer who built the Great Northern Railroad, replaced him. One of his major achievements was building and rebuilding the housing, cafeterias, hotels, water systems, repair shops, warehouses and other infrastructures needed by the thousands of incoming workers.

In 1907, Stevens resigned as chief engineer. His replacement, appointed by President Theodore Roosevelt, was U.S. Army Major George Washington Goethals of the U.S. Army Corps of Engineers (soon to be promoted to lieutenant colonel and later to colonel), a strong, United States Military Academy–trained leader and civil engineer. Goethals would direct the work in Panama to a successful conclusion.

Physically the Canal is a 50-mile waterway that connects the Atlantic Ocean with the Pacific. It has three locks on the Atlantic side that lift transiting vessels 85 feet high to Gatun Lake, where they steam under their own power across the lake to two more locks that drop them 85 feet to the level of the Pacific Ocean. This man-made miracle saves ships more than 8,000 miles were they to make the trip from Ocean to Ocean via the Cape of Good Hope at the Southern tip of South America.

During its 10-year construction (1904-1914), it was the most complicated structure ever built. Visitors from abroad by the thousands came, abetted by a personal visit by President Roosevelt himself in 1908, when a photograph of him at the controls of a giant steam shovel was published worldwide. Workers were divided in an interesting dichotomy. Skilled men, all white, mostly from America operated the steam shovels, dredges and railroad engines. Paid in US gold, they were known as "gold" employees. Laborers, mostly illiterate and multi-colored from places like Nicaragua, paid in local currencies were know as "silver" employees, although they earned far more than had they remained in their local countries.

In 1906, when troubles were casting doubts on the successful progress of work at the Canal site, Roosevelt decided to pay a 17-day visit to the site. It was the first time a sitting US President ever left the confines of the country. His visit made headlines, worldwide, and sparked new interest in the Canal. Teddy, a hyperactive visitor interested in everything surrounding him, often arrived at scheduled stops before his welcoming committees. On one occasion, skipping a fancy dinner at the local hotel, he took his thirty-cent meal at one of the "gold" employees local mess halls, bantering with his fellow Americans.

Digging, especially through what was known as the "culebra cut" the highest mountain range that ran north south through all the Americas, was the work of years. Several railroad lines ran the length of the project. Steam shovels were placed at intervals next to the railroad lines and as trains with empty cars approached, each steam shovel would drop its load of dirt onto the passing car. The trains ended up at where the Gatun Dam would be and dropped its load to create what would eventually become a giant dam. The Chagres River, which had earlier fed the Gatun Lake, had been dammed up until the digging was done, and then the small dams were exploded and the Chagres filled the lake.

Each lock was 1,000 feet long and 110 feet wide, which enabled the largest ship afloat in 1914 to enter each lock with ease. This engineering marvel used only gravity to lift each ship up to the level of Gatun Lake, and then, after traversing the Lake, drop the vessel down to the level of the other sea. Since Roosevelt had sent several photographers to record the construction, I found a rich treasure trove of still images to make my film.

Annual traffic has increased from about 1,000 ships when the Canal opened in 1914 to 14,702 vessels in 2008. And as supertankers and container ships have grown vastly in both length and width, there were thousands of ships too large to transit the Canal. Decades ago when the size of hundreds of new ships prevented their passage through the Canal, Panama decided to build a new set of locks, roughly double the size of the old, to accommodate these giant vessels. These new sets of locks will allow Panama to continue to service all the world's largest vessels.

Making this film gave me a sense of actually participating, in some small way, in what was certainly one of the most significant events of the last century. In am proud that I was able to display how this came about. I will conclude this chapter with this excerpt:

"The Panama Canal: History & Operation"
Produced & Directed by Sumner Jules Glimcher
http://youtu.be/ 3FseEz21x8

Dorice & Abe

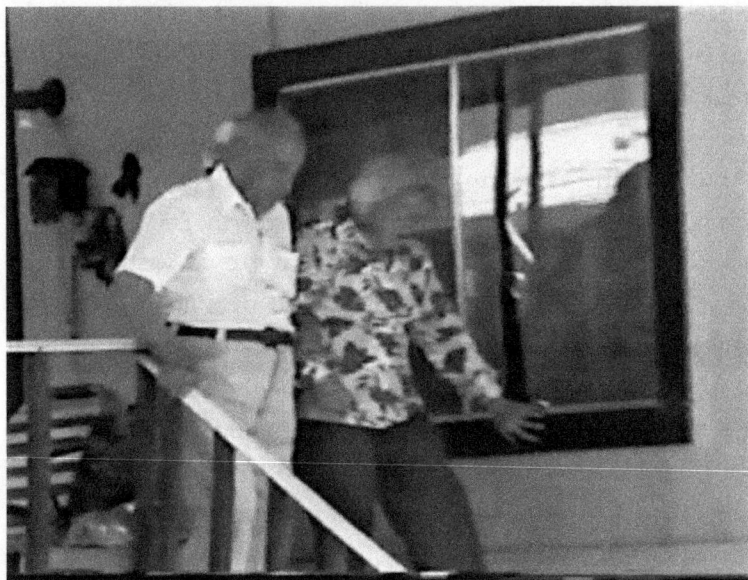

In a way, this format, what I call a 'Video Portrait,' is one of the most interesting forms I have ever made. It is a sort of 'this is your life' on video. So far in my entire career, I have just created only three, and this is the most intimate. It is the life of my mother when she was 93 years of age.

The other two were very different: an earlier chapter described the one I made for Ken Inadomi: **"John Kaichiro Inadomi: A Centennial Salute."** And more recently I created a video Portrait for a man named A. Alfred Taubman, commissioned by his children. One of the conditions of the latter was that I had to sign a secrecy agreement saying that it was just for his family and I was not allowed to show it to others.

Getting back to "**Dorice & Abe**," my mother was one of the most astonishing people I have ever known and one of her most outstanding characteristics was her incredible memory. I'll show you an example at the end of this chapter. Another was her zest for life. Yet another was the way in which she was able to adapt. Let's start with the latter.

When she was 84, her husband, my father, died of a heart attach at age 90. At that time she was working full time as a volunteer for the Muscular Dystrophy Association in Florida. That fact begins to tell you something about her and her values. Then my sister, Rosalie Harrington, living in Riverside, California told her that she must move to California to be closer to her. Since mom had very little income, Rosalie found her a subsidized flat for the elderly in Riverside, mom moved out there, and was comforted by the presence of her daughter.

A married couple that Rosalie knew, introduced mom to their elderly father, a man named Abe Stein, whose wife had recently died. He was then 91 and without his wife, whom had taken care of his every need, was totally lost without her. He had no idea of how to boil an egg, and lived with a service called, "meals on wheels" which delivered three meals a day to his small house. Abe flipped over meeting my mother. Call it need, call it love, call it loneliness call it whatever makes sense, he desperately wanted to marry her. Mom, who had been a totally independent soul, had severe doubts, but after months of pursuit, she finally acceded and they were married: he 91, she 84.

Flash forward nine years to when Abe had his 100th birthday and his three children gave him his 100th birthday party. Mother by then was 93. Invited to his birthday party, I flew to Riverside and brought along my video camera to record this unique event. Mother toasted Abe at the party saying that when many people asked her what the secret was to living to be one hundred, by saying that "You must be very careful, once you turn ninety-nine." She also had a great sense of humor.

After the party, which attracted over one hundred friends and relatives, I took them home and interviewed them both. They were very different. Mother, a woman of education, and culture who loved music, movies and theater was lost in a hick town without a theater or even a movie house, while Abe an ordinary but uneducated laborer who spent his working life in a piano factory, had little taste for the finer aspects of life. But somehow or other they had made a life together. When I interviewed them both, he had little to say, but she was articulate and had memories going back to when she was brought to America in 1900 at age five by her widowed mother. She remembered President McKinley's funeral when an anarchist assassinated him in 1901. She was totally amazing. So after several hours of interviews I pieced together a one-hour 'video portrait' that I made DVDs of and sent to my three children, who adored their grandma, and to all my living relatives. Every now and again I put the DVD into the player and there she is: as big as life!

When I was growing up, she told me that I could do anything I wanted to be, and do whatever I wanted. I believed her. And if I have achieved anything in my life, I am certain that she played a role in what I have achieved. Here is an example of her memory at 93.

"Dorice & Abe"
Produced & Directed by Sumner Jules Glimcher
http://youtu.be/9gEYCzHSnps

Here is an example of her sense of humor:

"Dorice & Abe"
Produced & Interviewed by Sumner Jules Glimcher
http://youtu.be/mCiusa7CYIc

Fable Safe

It was 1971, and it was the height of the cold war between the Soviet Union and the United States. Erik Barnouw and I were talking about what we could do at the Center for Mass Communication (CMC) at Columbia University to have an effect on the political climate at that time. We decided to create a shirt animated film: a sort of spoof on the term "Fail-Safe," and used as the title; "Fable-Safe." Erik wrote the words, in rhyme, and we asked our friend, the musician Tom Glazer to write music and sing. We had another friend, Robert Osborn who was, at that time, a highly successful political cartoonist to draw the images. And finally, Ted Nemeth, a Hungarian animation photographer, to take the pictures. I was the Producer, obtained the actual sound of the Hiroshima bomb, and put together the final explosion, which lasted almost half a minute, in the final sequence.

The film was the opening short for the New York Film Festival in 1971, and received a standing ovation when the nine-minute piece unspooled at Lincoln Center. It became an instant hit.

We did not use names of countries; it was always "we" and "they." When we talked about "we" we used images colored blue or black; "they" were always red. The first images were A-Bombs, then we upgraded to H-Bombs. We talked about MIRVs; (Multiple Independent Reentry Vehicles) "underground silos," "holes in the ground." A fabulous image of two soldiers whose eyeballs greatly enlarged protruded touching each other when the script said, "eyeballs to eyeballs." Terms such as "balance of terror" & "deterrent credibility" were tossed around. We showed animated protestors carrying peace signs show as the script said, "Whatever happened to patriotism?" And finally, when we talked about "first strikes" and see images on radar that might (or might not be flocks of geese or mallard ducks) we see a finger on a red button that puts us into the final sequence.

Since the film is great fun and only nine minutes, here it is in its entirety.

"Fable Safe"
Executive Producer Sumner Jules Glimcher
http://youtu.be/orSPoAS4xwM

Filmography & Awards

Filmography

TITLE	DATE	SPONSOR
A. Alfred Taubman: A Video Portrait	2009	Taubman Family
A Taste of Provence: Art, Culture & History	2006	Westminster Productions
The Evolution of Unitarianism	2005	The Unitarian Church
In the Shadow if the Vampire	2004	The Unitarian Church
The Panama Canal: History & Operation	2004	Westminster Productions
September 2001: A Personal Memoir	2002	NBC Network
John Kaiichiro Inadomi: 1897-1997	1997	Inadomi Family
Dorice & Abe	1990	Westminster Productions
Introduction to Japan: (Filmstrips)	1990	Harvard University

TITLE	DATE	SPONSOR
China, Old and New (Filmstrips)	1978	Harvard University
Old World, New Women	1975	Taiwan Consulate
Confucius	1975	Taiwan Consulate
UN Heads of State (audio cassettes)	1973	Mass Communications
Masterpieces of Chinese Art	1972	Taiwan Consulate
Golden Heritage, Golden Harvest	1972	Taiwan Consulate
New Their Home is Israel	1971	Hadassah
Hiroshima-Nagasaki, Aug. 1945	1970	Center for Mass Communications
Fable Safe	1970	Center for Mass Communications
North from Mexico	1969	Greenwood Press
A Problem of Power	1968	National Council of Churches
Alberto Giacometti	1967	Center for Mass Communications
Memento	1966	AT&T

TITLE	DATE	SPONSOR
Project Haystack (Radio Telescope)	1965	M.I.T.'s Lincoln Labs
Planting	1964	Brooklyn Botanical Gardens
Eric Bentley	1963	PBS
Eero Saarinen, Architect	1962	PBS

Awards

Recipient of more than three dozen major national and international awards, including: Golden Mercury, Venice; First Prize and Grand Prize, Vienna; Special Diploma, Zagreb; Gold Medal, Atlanta; Trophy Award, Salerno; Silver Dragon, Kracow; Chris Award, Columbus; awards at Edinburgh, Rio de Janeiro, Varna, Antwerp, Tel Aviv, Brno; Awards of Merit, National Committee of Films for Safety, American Horticultural Film Festival; multiple CINE Golden Eagles and American Film Festival Blue Ribbons.

About The Author

Sumner Jules Glimcher, Professor Emeritus from NYU has worked in film, radio and television since he was graduated from Harvard with a degree in nuclear physics in 1948. He began his career as a Page at NBC in New York where, in six years, he worked with many of the greats in the Golden Age of Television; Sid Caesar, Carl Reiner, Neil Simon, et al, advancing rapidly in production and operations as television grew from four hours daily to eighteen. Then followed three years at Radio Free Europe in Munich during which time he travelled widely throughout all of western Europe. Working with the BBC in England, the RAI in Italy, and the government of Portugal where RFE's long wave transmitters were located, allowed him to to learn about all the technical aspects of international broadcasting. Returning to the United States in 1958 he created International Transmissions, Inc. (ITI), the first independent international voiced news service for radio and television, the precursor of CNN, bringing live news reports from all around the world to U.S. broadcasters. Subsequently he joined WOR and RKO General in New York as Manager of Foreign News, where in addition to putting the first space shot on television, he also covered the inauguration of John F. Kennedy on location. In 1962 he went to work for National Educational Television, now known as the Public Broadcasting Service, where he was in charge of bringing programs from abroad to the United States. He was the first broadcaster to initiate a program exchange with NHK in Japan, and imported the first documentaries from the National Film Board of Canada, the Canadian Broadcasting Corporation, and the Norddeutsche Rundfunk in Germany.

He began his academic career in 1963 when he was hired by Columbia University as the Manager of the Center for Mass Communication, a unit devoted to the production and distribution of educational films. Shortly thereafter, he began to teach, ultimately becoming Deputy Chairman of the Department of Radio and Television in Columbia's Graduate School of the Arts. He wrote his first book, *"MOVIE MAKING: A GUIDE TO FILM PRODUCTION"* published by Simon & Schuster's Pocketbook Division in paper, which sold over 25,000 copies and became required reading in a number of film schools, including NYU. The book was also published in hardcover by Columbia University Press. During that period he met and recorded a series of interviews with Frances Flaherty, widow of Robert *"Nanook of the North"* Flaherty, and programmed the International Flaherty Film Seminars for two years.

After a decade-long tenure (1962-1972) at Columbia, he resigned to form his own production company, Mass Communications, Incorporated, in 1972, which enabled him to continue making educational and documentary films, In the early 1970's, he developed a close working relationship with Harvard, his alma mater and created several series of programs on China with John King Fairbank, and several on Japan with Edwin O. Reischauer, at which time he began his extensive travels to East Asia.

In the late 1970's, he was recruited by the Consulate General of Japan to serve as Film Consultant, helping to inform America about Japan through the broadcast of Japanese films that were shown on American television stations; an activity he continued for twenty years. He spent academic 1977/78 in Cambridge when Harvard's President Derek Bok appointed him a Consultant and asked him to undertake a one-year study and report on the use of media in education. In June, 1978 he completed an 82 page report, recommending that Harvard establish a Video Production Center and put its outstanding faculty on videotape.

Two trips to Taiwan (one in 1973; the other in 1975) resulted in four films, and that work, along with his consultancy for the Japanese and his work with Fairbank and Reischauer made him a frequent visitor to East Asia. As a result of his knowledge of East Asia, he began to show his slides and films and lecture on China and Japan and led groups of filmmakers and photographers to China, Japan and Hong Kong. He subsequently became a lecturer on eleven cruises (including two for Princess Lines, one for the Harvard Alumni Association, one for Holland American, two for Crystal Cruises, several for Celebrity, amongst others). He has also been a Consultant to the United Nations and several private institutions. In 1998 he was named the Director of the Department of Film, Video and Broadcasting at New York University's School of Continuing Education where he helped create one of the finest film schools on the east coast.

After his early retirement from NYU in 1996 at age 72, he established and became the President of Westminster Productions, Inc., where he continues his professional activities. He created the series of film screenings titled, "Meet The Filmmaker" wherein he screens independent documentaries on a regular basis for NATAS (National Academy of Television Arts & Sciences). He is a member of the Harvard Club of New York; and The Dutch Treat Club for which he serves as a member of the Board of Governors and also on the Speakers Committee. He is also a member of the Overseas Press Club and the Foreign Press Association. He has just completed his memoir titled, "A Filmmaker's Journal." It is currently available on Amazon in a variety of formats. He currently lives in New York City. For more information about the author, please visit: www.sumnerjulesglimcher.com

www.ingramcontent.com/pod-product-compliance
Lightning Source LLC
Chambersburg PA
CBHW031535040426
42445CB00010B/556